A FINE BALANCE: ASSESSING THE QUALITY OF GOVERNANCE IN BOTSWANA

EDITED BY KARIN ALEXANDER AND GAPE KABOYAKGOSI

idasa
AN AFRICAN DEMOCRACY INSTITUTE

2012

EMBASSY OF DENMARK

Idasa wishes to thank the Embassy of Denmark for its funding of this project.

Published by Idasa, 357 Visagie Street, Pretoria 0001

© Idasa 2012

ISBN 978-1-920409-77-7

First published 2012

Editing by Paul Wise

Design, layout and production by Bronwen Müller

Cover by Mandy Darling

CONTENTS   PAGE

Acronyms and Abbreviations   v

Foreword   1

Introduction   2
    Botswana's great democratic story   2
    The characteristics of a minimalist democracy   3
    Grounds for future contestation   8

The Index: 100 questions contextualising Botswana's democracy   14

Section One: Participation and Democracy   24
    Nationhood   26
    Participation and Involvement   29
    Government legitimacy   30
    Citizenship obligations and duties   32
    Tolerance   32
    Conclusion   33

Section Two: Elections and Democracy   34
    Elections   35
    Equal votes   38
    Open competition   39
    Election rules   41
    Voter information   43
    Electoral participation   46
    Electoral outcomes   48
    Funding elections   50
    Conclusion   52

Section Three: Accountability and Democracy   53
    Executive accountability and legislative oversight   54
    Public participation and accountability   56
    Law-making and the budget process   59
    Access to information   60
    Accessibility and independence   60
    Conclusion   63

Section Four: Political freedoms and democracy   65

    Civil and political rights   67

    Freedom of association and participation   72

    Political parties   75

    Media rights   77

    Conclusion   80

Section Five: Human dignity and democracy   83

    Socio-economic rights protection   85

    Reasonable access to clean and adequate water   87

    Adequate food   88

    Adequate shelter and housing   89

    Adequate and unimpeded access to land   90

    Health care   91

    Education   93

    Poverty   94

    Jobs and rights in the workplace   96

    Delivery of social and economic rights   96

    Corporate governance   97

    Conclusion and recommendations   98

Biographical Information   100

References   102

ACRONYMS AND ABBREVIATIONS

ART	antiretroviral therapy
BALA	Botswana Association of Local Authorities
BDC	Botswana Development Corporation
BDF	Botswana Defence Force
BESnet	Botswana Electoral Support Network
BIDPA	Botswana Institute for Development Policy Analysis
BOCONGO	Botswana Council of Non-Governmental Organisations
BOFEPUSO	Botswana Federation of Public Employees Organisations
BOFEPUSU	Botswana Federation of Public Sector Unions
BONELA	Botswana Network on Ethics, Law and HIV/Aids
CEDA	Citizen Entrepreneurial Development Agency
CEDAW	Convention on the Elimination of all forms of Discrimination Against Women
CESCR	(United Nations) Committee on Economic, Social and Cultural Rights
CRC	(United Nations) Convention on the Rights of the Child
DISS	Directorate of Intelligence and Security Services
DPSM	Directorate of Public Service Management
DWA	Department of Water Affairs
EU	European Union
FPTP	first past the post
HLCC	High Level Consultative Council
ICC	International Criminal Court
ICESCR	International Covenant on Economic, Social and Cultural Rights
IEC	Independent Electoral Commission
ILO	International Labour Organisation
JSC	Judicial Service Commission
LEA	Local Enterprise Authority
LeGaBiBo	Lesbian, Gays and Bisexuals of Botswana
LSB	Law Society of Botswana
MFDP	Ministry of Finance and Development Planning
MISA	Media Institute of Southern Africa
MMEWR	Ministry of Minerals, Energy and Water Affairs
NGO	Non-Governmental Organisation
OECD	Organisation of Economic Cooperation and Development
PLWHA	people living with HIV and AIDS
SACU	Southern African Customs Union
SADC	Southern African Development Community
SHHA	Self-Help Housing Agency
UDHR	Universal Declaration on Human Rights
UN	United Nations
WUC	Water Utilities Corporation

BOTSWANA'S POLITICAL PARTIES

BAM	Botswana Alliance Movement
BCP	Botswana Congress Party
BDP	Botswana Democratic Party
BIP	Botswana Independence Party
BMD	Botswana Movement for Democracy
BNF	Botswana National Front
BPP	Botswana People's Party
BPU	Botswana Progressive Union
IFP	Independence Freedom Party
MELS	Marx, Engels, Lenin, Stalin Movement
NDF	National Democratic Front

FOREWORD

Idasa developed the Democracy Index to assess the depth of democracy in South Africa. In its initial iteration, designed by Robert Mattes and Richard Calland, the Index comprised 150 questions. These were honed to a list of 100 questions in 2005 and the same questions were used for Idasa's most recent South Africa Democracy Index in 2010. The research relies on expert analysis to answer a set of questions that interrogate how closely, in practice, democracy meets the broad ideal of self-representative government. More specifically, to what extent can citizens control elected officials and government appointees who make decisions about public affairs; and, how equal are citizens to one another in this accountability process? To provide a more detailed appraisal, the Democracy Index assesses a country through five focus areas: participation, elections, accountability, political freedoms, and human dignity.

Idasa is in the process of expanding the Index into Southern Africa in an effort to broaden the capacity of individuals and organisations monitoring and supporting democratic governance efforts in the sub-region. As the Idasa Democracy Index is tested in a range of Southern African countries, the tool will be enhanced and nationalised. The hope is that citizens of any country can use the Democracy Index to assess and debate the current state of its democracy. The purpose of the scores is to assist citizens in making their own judgements, based on the information made available, to stimulate national debate and to provide democracy promoters with a tool for identifying issues and needs that can be addressed by education, advocacy, training, institution building and policy revision. This is the inaugural Index for Botswana and is intended to set a benchmark for democracy to be measured against in the future.

All of the authors selected to contribute, as well as one of the co-editors, are based in Botswana and/or are Batswana. Together, their depth of expertise is grounded in years devoted to activism, civil society, academia and government. Authors were asked to provide a numerical score for each question and a narrative justifying their rating. The group convened twice in 2011 to ensure both a common understanding of the Index and peer review of the ongoing assessment process. The second of these meetings took the form of a validation workshop at which other members of civil society, academia and government were invited to give feedback and comment on the analysis. While authors were requested to consult other indices and to reflect the opinions of an expert reference group, ultimately this is an individual expert assessment. As such, each set of Democracy Index results stands on its own and is not suitable for statistical comparison across years or cross-country comparative ranking.

It is through its use by Batswana that the Idasa Democracy Index can enhance research capacity, assist representative groups to lobby for greater democratic depth and quality, and spark participatory engagement between governments and citizens. Idasa is grateful to its in-country partners for their willingness to try out the tool, their commitment to the process and the ongoing work on democracy that they do as individuals or through their organisations.

Karin Alexander – Team Leader: Measuring and Monitoring Democracy, Idasa

INTRODUCTION

BY GAPE KABOYAKGOSI & KENEILWE MARATA

This Introduction has several aims, the first of which is to set out evidence affirming Botswana's credentials as a democracy. It goes on to demonstrate that Botswana is actually a minimalist democracy: a system that does as little as possible to engender participation, transparency, access to social support, accountability and human rights, among other things. It then notes emerging calls for change based on persistent signs of disagreement with the status quo. The importance of these is their multiplicity of tactics and broadness of base, putting in question the image of Botswana as a stable democracy. Thereafter this chapter points the way forward by predicting some future areas of contestation, which include the Constitution, socio-economic issues, governance and corruption.

BOTSWANA'S GREAT DEMOCRATIC STORY

Botswana is a multi-party democracy, having held elections every five years since 1966, when it received independence from the UK. It is Africa's oldest and most consistent democracy in that respect. The strength of democracy in Botswana has been recognised in many ways: in 2008, for instance, the Mo Ibrahim Foundation awarded a former president, Festus Mogae, the Ibrahim Prize for excellence as a Head of State,[1] and even before that the country had been elected to the Security Council of the United Nations. Botswana has also experienced three presidential changes, all within a legal, constitutional framework.

Numerous governance indicators show Botswana performing well. In the World Bank's Worldwide Governance Indicators, Botswana is given very high ratings for sub-indicators such as 'government effectiveness', 'regulatory quality', 'political stability', 'rule of law' and 'control of corruption': the country consistently scores in the upper quartiles, with the exception of 'voice and accountability', which has demonstrated worrying declines (*see* Moatlhaping & Moletsane in this volume). The Ibrahim Index of African Governance, which is dedicated to promoting good governance in Africa, also shows Botswana consistently in the top three performers on the continent in terms of good governance (sub-indicators include 'participation and human rights', 'rule of law', 'transparency and corruption', 'safety and security', 'sustainable economic opportunity' and 'human development').[2] In terms of ethical governance, Transparency International's Corruption Perceptions Index has awarded Botswana top place in Africa since 1996.[3]

To facilitate accountability, the Botswana government operates on the separation-of-powers model, with the three branches of government – legislature, judiciary and executive – relatively independent of one another. To facilitate decentralisation, Botswana has 16 district councils, of which six are urban and ten rural. These councils are statutory entities, but not constitutionally enshrined. Yet, while functioning by and large as extensions of central implementation capacity, they serve to deepen local democratic culture as their members are elected directly by people in their localities.

Botswana also observes human rights. The citizens enjoy certain freedoms, enshrined in the Constitution, that are often termed 'first-generation rights', such as the right to freedom of association, the right to life and the right to freedom of movement (*see* Mogwe & Melville in this volume). Botswana also ensures that civil society enjoys many freedoms, such as the freedom to operate in the country without hindrance or harassment by the State (Maundeni 2005). From the registration of societies to their day-to-day operations, there is minimal State interference (Kaunda 2008).

With its economy heavily dependent on diamonds, another well-documented characteristic of Botswana is that the nation consistently invests diamond revenues into extensive social expenditure for the protection of less affluent members of society. This makes Botswana one of the highest per capita spenders on education in Africa, and its figures for access to health, education and water are probably among the highest on the continent too. For instance, 85% of the population are within a five-kilometre radius of a health facility and 96% have access to healthy drinking water. The government also provides free, universal access to antiretroviral drugs to members of the population with HIV and AIDS. Furthermore, a 12-year education is free and universal in Botswana (Vision Council 2009).

THE CHARACTERISTICS OF A MINIMALIST DEMOCRACY

That Botswana is a democracy is not in question. However, the challenge lies in agreeing on the quality or depth of the democracy. Critics of the system, such as Kenneth Good, have termed it 'authoritarian liberalism' (Good 1996). Similarly Botlhomilwe *et al.* (2011)

question the depth of the democracy and argue that the quality of Botswana as Africa's democratic success story is questionable. However, we prefer to characterise it as minimalist. The term 'minimalist democracy' is used to describe a democratic system in which the main defining characteristic is the certainty of free, credible elections being held (McElhenny 2004). It is therefore a term used to connote democracies with perceived shortcomings. A democracy characterised as minimalist lacks the characteristic of facilitating broad-based participation (see Moatlhaping & Moletsane in this volume). It is this shortcoming, coupled with the obvious adherence to electoral democracy, that allows us to apply this label to Botswana.

On one front, while the system is praised for its minimal interference with civil society operations, it also does the minimum to ensure the strengthening of civil society. One example is that while a civil society policy was adopted by parliament in 2002 (Government of Botswana 2002), to date it has not been put into practice, leaving relations between civil society and the State largely undefined and thus State-centred. A perusal of the policy shows, further, that the State has overlooked the fact that civil society organisations exist for reasons other than service delivery – for example, as pressure groups. The fact that the State prefers to see these organisations as agents of service delivery, and will only work with them if they are registered with the State, betrays a bias towards those elements of civil society that can be controlled by the government (Government of Botswana 2002). For instance, the government recently refused to register the organisation Lesbian, Gays and Bisexuals of Botswana (LeGaBiBo). This means that, because the law forbids homosexuality in Botswana, LeGaBiBo cannot deliver services to its constituency, even though that constituency certainly does exist.

The government of Botswana generally observes accountability (see Botlhale in this volume), but here 'accountability' is defined minimally. State-owned corporations, until 2011, had to account to parliament only indirectly, in that such accounting was made mainly to ministers and not directly to parliament (Kaboyakgosi 2011). As for political accountability, a peculiarity of Botswana is the lack of recourse for voters: there is no method of recall for representatives who are deemed inefficient. Voters have to wait for five years to recall such representatives (see Mokgosi in this volume). There is also a huge resource asymmetry among the political parties (Molomo & Sebudubudu 2005). The two top leaders of the ruling party, the president and his deputy, have the advantage of being covered by State television on all missions they undertake, whether political campaigns or official State business. Opposition functionaries have no such access (see Mokgosi in this volume).

More evidence of minimalist accountability is that the government continues to frustrate reforms that would prevent wrongdoing, such as laws on the declaration of assets by leaders, despite parliament having passed such a law in 2003 (see Ndlovu in this volume). There is also no law to protect public-minded officials or citizens wishing to expose wrongdoing. Whistle-blower protection legislation has been discussed many times, but to no avail. Similarly, the government seems reluctant to institute a freedom of information law, which would support the public's right of access of information. Such laws would ordinarily improve transparency and go some way in reducing corruption. The government is now drafting these measures (see Botlhale in this volume), though their effect might yet be diluted by a raft of other laws whose application will further erode access to information. These include the Media Practitioners Act (2009), the Intelligence and Security Act (2007) and the National Security Act (1986) (*see* Ndlovu in this volume). Indeed, to the government's chagrin, Botswana received the dubious 'Golden Padlock' award from the Media Institute of Southern Africa in recognition of this tendency to secrecy.

Batswana are widely thought to see democratic methods as the only valid way to change governments (*see* Moatlhaping & Moletsane in this volume), with the last elections having recorded a most impressive turnout (*see* Mokgosi in this volume). There is nevertheless a qualification with regard to wide voter turnout: a closer look reveals that turnout is meas-ured in terms of the proportion of registered voters who cast their ballots on voting day. If measured according to the number of eligible voters casting a ballot, turnout would be lower. Considering this in conjunction with the extremely low turnout for national referendums, it is arguable that participation in elections in Botswana is lower than it appears (Vision Council 2010a).

While political parties both build and institutionalise democracy (Molomo 2008:121), a worrying trend in Botswana is apparent in the continual allegations of lack of internal democracy in political parties. The parties do not seem to fully embrace contestation for party position (*see* Ndlovu in this volume). With the exception, perhaps, of the Botswana National Front, whose contests for party positions are robust to the extent of regularly caus-ing the break-up of the party, there is a reluctance to deepen democratic practice within political parties. For instance, of the four political parties with a parliamentary presence that have held congresses since 2009, such congresses have been instructive in one regard: the lack of opposition in electoral contests or the deliberate selection of candidates by means other than electoral. The ruling Botswana Democratic Party (BDP) selected its central com-mittee members on the basis of what they termed 'compromise': the party chairman was mandated by the president to collect the names of interested people, which were later put up for endorsement by the congress. No contest for any position was held. The Botswana Congress Party (BCP) had only Dumelang Salashando, their party president, as presidential candidate, while the newly formed Botswana Movement for Democracy (BMD) had seri-ous contests for the presidential seats only where Sidney Pilane lost against Gomolemo Motswaledi (*see* Ndlovu in this volume). While preaching democracy, political parties, it seems, do not like to practise it internally.

The habit of not extending democratic practice to the citizenry also exists on the eco-nomic management front, where fiscal policy involves minimal participation. Until 2010, which saw the adoption of the practice of budget *dipitso* (traditional forums), Members of Parliament, civil society and the media only got to see the budget the day the Minister of Finance announced it (*see* Botlhale in this volume). The lack of transparency in Botswana has led to its decline on the Open Budget Index (Kaboyakgosi 2011). While this Index mainly measures the expenditure side of the budget, the revenue aspect is no more trans-parent. The per-carat value of diamonds, Botswana's major foreign exchange earner, is not revealed, even to Members of Parliament (Magang 2008).

Before the advent of the budget *dipitso*, the public budget did not carry a pre-budget statement, which made it difficult for outsiders to understand the parameters that the gov-ernment used to allocate public finance. While legislators were expected to comment on the

budget, not understanding its parameters made their task almost redundant: the executive would have had nearly a year to prepare the budget and the legislature just a month to interrogate it. While the budget *dipitso* represents a healthy break from past practices of lack of transparency in budgeting, challenges persist, particularly in that Botswana's budget still lacks a tracking mechanism to assess the veracity of expenditure in relation to the budget.

Other challenges to Botswana's democracy include the extremely low representation of women in the national political arena (*see* Mokgosi in this volume, and Ntseane & Sentsho 2005) and the low participation of youth in politics (Ntsabane 2005). While the role of women in positions of decision-making in major institutions has improved (Vision Council 2010), the same cannot be said about political positions, with only four women in the current parliament, two of whom are specially elected. Several reasons have been suggested for this state of affairs, including the patriarchal nature of society (Kaboyakgosi 2003) and the resource differential between males and females.

Human rights are another area of concern. Although Botswana is not known for flagrant abuse of human rights, there are some practices that cause concern, among them the death penalty (*see* Mogwe & Melville in this volume). Added to this is the reluctance of the State to provide institutional infrastructure to support the protection of human rights. Botswana still does not have a human rights commission, unlike some other countries in the region, including Malawi, Namibia and South Africa. The Office of the Ombudsman, which ought to undertake the protection of human rights, is overly concerned with civil service matters and, critically, has been ignored by the executive when it has raised uncomfortable questions (*see* Ndlovu in this volume).

While Botswana is a good performer in terms of economic indicators, large income inequalities are part and parcel of the country's politics. The State has continually supported the weakest in society and provided support in the form of social support mechanisms (Seleka *et al.* 2007), including assisted programmes for ploughing and livestock rearing, food baskets for the poor and old-age pensions. What concerns civil society, however, is the lack of constitutional protection of these mechanisms (*see* Mogwe & Melville in this volume). For instance, while access to water is widespread, meaning that Botswana has surpassed its obligations in terms of the Millennium Development Goals, and access to health care is similarly impressive, it remains a fact that there are no obligations on the State to provide these forms of assistance. It is therefore possible that social spending could be one of the areas to suffer when fiscal means are strained.

Its status as a democratic nation notwithstanding, Botswana's democratic consensus is disintegrating. As is characteristic of Botswana's political culture of negotiation and traditions of dialogue, the way in which this is occurring is without open, overt attrition.[4] In the past few years, several occurrences attest to this disintegration, including legal challenges to the status quo, the break-up of political parties, labour unrest and international action over unfair but long-standing practices that exist within the democracy. Botswana has endured situations of open discontent before, even resulting in constitutional reforms. We argue, however, that what makes the current discontent different is that it is sustained, that it is occurring in many arenas (for example, locally and abroad), and that it entails many different tactics. For instance, civil society organisations that challenge the State can now join international partners or take Botswana to the United Nations. In other words, besides just using the judicial system or lobbying the State through its own preferred mechanisms, civil society is increasingly using mechanisms likely to make the State take serious note of their concerns.

It has long been assumed that Botswana's stability is due to its ethnic heterogeneity. Without calling for separatism, many of Botswana's tribes are demanding ethnic equality before the law, including access to land and equality of language. Fundamental to the idea of eight main tribes was that tribes physically located in the geographical areas of the so-called main tribes were automatically identified as belonging to those main tribes. However, this status is being questioned vigorously. Ethnic identity is being renegotiated, with the traditionally minor tribes challenging the status quo. Sections 77, 78 and 79 of the Constitution have been amended in the face of growing disenchantment by ethnic groups in Botswana. The essential effect of the amendment is to give the minor tribes representation in the House of Chiefs.

Matters involving dissatisfaction in relation to language are persisting. The Wayeyi, one of the so-called minority groups, took the government to a United Nations commission on culture (*see* Ndlovu in this volume). Other issues include a court case by the Basarwa (San) against the government (*see* Ndlovu in this volume). The Basarwa won the case, in which they were seeking to be allowed to reside in the Central Kalahari Game Reserve. The case is instructive for two reasons: the Basarwa, Botswana's smallest tribe, fought the case not only locally, but also internationally, by allying themselves with Survival International, a global minority rights advocacy group. Probably more effectively, they also threatened to target Botswana diamonds by threatening an alliance with Hollywood actors, something that a government minister called 'unpatriotic'!

Botswana's conservative society is confronting an increasingly assertive gay and lesbian community. For many years dismissed as 'forbidden', these sexual minorities have a court case pending against the government. What makes this more significant is not only that it would have been unheard of only a decade or so ago, but also that the case has the support of none other than a former president of Botswana, Festus Mogae, who has consistently called for the liberalisation of attitudes towards sexuality and openly championed the idea of decriminalising homosexual relationships. To show how serious the matter was, when asked why he had not led such calls during his presidency, Mogae answered that he had not wanted to lose an election. He also called for the decriminalising of prostitution, an equally controversial issue in Botswana's conservative society.

On the party-political front, an issue of note in the history of Botswana was the break-up of the BDP. The party's stability as an institution is arguably one of the factors that led to Botswana's stability (*see* Ndlovu in this volume). Prior to 2010, it was Botswana's opposition that was prone to fragmentation (Kaunda 2008), which was blamed for the poor performance of the opposition in electoral contests. The ruling BDP, on the other hand, had never split, even though it had endured some robust factional attrition. The disagreements

leading to the break-up included quarrels over the president's perceived unfairness in supporting one faction over the other and his unwillingness to recognise a new central committee. Gomolemo Motswaledi, who was elected secretary-general of the BDP in the ill-fated central committee that President Khama refused to recognise, later went on to challenge the president in court, where he lost with costs: Botswana's Constitution forbids the challenging of presidential powers and decisions.[5] These disagreements within the BDP were amplified in a public campaign for financial contributions in aid of Motswaledi's case. The organisers of the appeal spoke of a broad-based campaign cutting across political lines: members of the BDP are alleged to have been among the contributors.

Fissures are also emerging between traditional leaders and the government. The *dikgosi* (traditional leaders), often labelled as enforcers of BDP rule (Vaughn 2003), are now challenging the government more often and more publicly. Traditionally, skirmishes between the House of Chiefs and the government were largely restricted to individual *dikgosi* and did not involve the leaders collectively. Kgosi Seepapitso of the Bangwaketse and Kgosi Linchwe of the Bakgatla were most prominent in publicly expressing views contrary to those of the State. That form of disagreement still prevails, as exemplified by Kgosi Mosadi Seboko's recent refusal to toe the government's line when he met with striking public servants. A bigger issue is perhaps the recent, very public voicing of displeasure by the *dikgosi* collectively over what they termed the government's lack of consultation with them on the suspension of Kgosi Kgafela. Another is their refusal to endorse the government's motion on floor-crossing by political representatives.

On another front, Botswana's labour relations, previously assumed to be cordial, became fractious in 2011. In 2010 the law forbidding strike action was changed, allowing trade unions to strike, which is exactly what happened in 2011. While Botswana had long been praised for its tranquil labour relations, the strike brought home an uncomfortable truth: neither the government nor the trade unions were prepared to handle such a momentous national matter. On the State-owned television station, BTV, mainly government officials were interviewed, thus depriving the public of the views of labour. Importantly, though, the private media were carrying stories of the strike from the unions' point of view. While the private media did, belatedly, cover the government's side, a pattern was established: that the State media were mainly about the government and the private media about the unions.

It is therefore evident that, beneath the stability the country has enjoyed, there have been multiple sources of discontent: labour law, ethnic relations, lack of internal party democracy, traditional leaders' dissatisfaction with their location in this modern democracy and others. These causes of conflict, previously latent, are now being actively addressed by citizens.

GROUNDS FOR FUTURE CONTESTATION

This discussion is based on ongoing challenges to State hegemony. Notwithstanding the stability associated with Botswana, there are disagreements that are growing in both range and volume. They show Batswana to be taking an increasingly active role in the everyday life of their democracy.

The following are issues likely to cause more friction between the nation's leaders and its citizens.

THE ECONOMY AND SOCIETY

Part of the Botswana story has been about the redistribution of mineral revenues to offset poverty. As in other respects, the government received much credit for ensuring that its citizens did not starve. However, Botswana's economic base, which relies on high productivity and returns from diamonds, is under threat, as is citizen participation in the economy.

- There are indications that the South African government may want to revise the revenue-sharing formula of the Southern African Customs Union (SACU). SACU revenues form a significant portion of Botswana's national revenues and revision of the formula could result in lower revenues for Botswana, thus putting more pressure on Botswana's macro-economic situation (Grynberg & Motswapong, forthcoming).

- The economy is diversifying too slowly, challenging the capacity of the State to continue sustaining the country's poor (Vision Council 2010a).

- The traditionally participative cattle industry is coming under pressure because the European Union (EU) has shown reluctance to buy beef where cattle are not traceable. Future ramifications may lead to reduced participation, especially by citizens without farms, pushing many into the economic margins. Already the EU has suspended buying beef from Botswana due to inadequate standards of hygiene at the Botswana Meat Commission.

- Most citizens are neither saving for the future nor able to participate in the stock exchange.

- The government's attempts to alleviate poverty seem to have failed to ensure that recipients of social support graduate from poverty. While the government has many schemes to alleviate poverty, these have not demonstrated any record of lifting recipients out of poverty. The poor are perpetually so.

The overall implication is that the government might come under pressure if the economy continues to perform poorly. Poor economic performance would in turn compromise the government's ability to make transfers to the poor, leading to less participation by poor people in national life.

RISING PERCEPTIONS OF CORRUPTION AND CORPORATE GOVERNANCE LAPSES

Commitment to clean governance, another of Botswana's trademarks, is under threat and could lead to more questions being asked of the government. While Botswana continues to perform well in managing corruption, indicators show Botswana actually declining compared with the rest of the world (Vision Council 2009; Kaunda 2008). Events that might cast doubt on Botswana's commitment to clean governance include the following.

- Minister Ndelu Seretse resigned from the Cabinet amid allegations of a conflict of interest. He won the subsequent legal battle to clear his name.

- Minister of Finance and Development Planning, Kenneth Mathambo, did not resign from the Cabinet when facing similar allegations, and he won the subsequent legal case.

- Former Assistant Minister of Finance and Development Planning, Samson Guma Moyo, left the Cabinet under similar suspicions.

- There has been an increase in allegations of wrongdoing by leaders of State-owned corporations, including the Botswana Export Development and Investment Authority and the Botswana Development Corporation (BDC), where forensic audits have revealed mismanagement. Parliament intends to carry out investigations at the BDC in conjunction with those by the Directorate on Corruption and Economic Crime.

- There has been a successful court challenge to the awarding of a tender for the construction of the government-funded Botswana Innovation Hub.

None of these ministers or chief executives have been convicted of anything, and there have also been other allegations of corruption in the highest places. The prosecution of these allegations might signal that the government is prepared to deal with corruption; a failure to prosecute would compromise the image of the country as a State with clean governance.

Another area of concern would be the failure of the government to institute a law to facilitate the declaration of assets by senior government officials, including ministers. Failing to introduce such a measure would allow such instances as those decribed above to continue. A law to facilitate the declaration of assets by national leaders would not only help place them above suspicion, but would also lead to more ethical governance and help protect the image of the country.

Constitutional reforms

The Vision Council's survey of citizens in 2010 showed that 72% desired constitutional review in Botswana (Vision Council 2010a). Now, more than ever, citizens are questioning Botswana's Constitution. Calls for change have been made in the past – in *Unity Dow v The Attorney General*, among other cases – for the reduction of voting age, the limitation of presidential terms, voting by proxy and other reforms (Phirinyane *et. al.* 2004). Calls for constitutional reforms are not new, but there are signs that these calls are increasing. In many cases there has been little resistance from the State, but new calls being made may be difficult to implement, leading to more friction between the State and society. Many causes of disagreement still exist, including the following:

- Sections of the nation are questioning the constitutional arrangement that provides for a vice president to automatically become president when a sitting president leaves the position.

- Opposition political parties are constantly calling for reforms to the electoral law, especially to change from the current first-past-the-post (FPTP) system to proportional representation.

- Bakgatla paramount chief Kgosi Kgafela is challenging the validity of the Constitution on the grounds that it was adopted without sufficient consultation with citizens.

- Sections of society are unhappy with presidential immunity, since a court case involving President Khama and former BDP secretary-general Gomolemo Motswaledi confirmed that the president was immune from prosecution (*see* Ndlovu in this volume).

- Sections of society disagree with the practice of specially elected Members of Parliament and councillors.

- A court case challenging the criminalisation of homosexuality is on the way (*see* Ndlovu in this volume).

The fact that the people making these calls are from a range of different persuasions will make for contentious debates. For instance, those who advocate the recognition of gay rights (a very liberal perspective in Botswana) might not necessarily be in favour of giving more powers to *dikgosi* (a very conservative institution). Even within the opposition party ranks, activists seem divided on the merits of the matter.[6] The battle lines are thus drawn: for the foreseeable future, Botswana appears set for sustained periods of wrangling over the Constitution.

A NEW TURN IN BOTSWANA'S GOVERNANCE

The government of Botswana has, to date, been in a position to set the terms of engagement with non-State actors, often excluding those it does not wish to deal with. However, the State is losing some of its capacity to do this. Other actors are finding ways to enter the policy arena using means previously less explored.

- The role of the private media in setting the agenda, and in giving alternative perspectives to State media, is growing, challenging the State's hegemony.

- The implementation of the Media Practitioners Act (2009), which requires a legal practitioner appointed by the Law Society of Botswana (LSB), has been stymied because the LSB has not put forward one of its members.

- Employing a tactic likely to be used more frequently, the LSB threatened to report the government to the International Criminal Court (ICC) over the public's unease at the government's handling of matters related to extra-judicial killings. The threat to report the government was apparently defused after the then Minister for Justice and Security, Ndelu Seretse, met with the LSB (*see* Ndlovu in this volume).

- Trade unions have taken on an increasingly political role. During the 2009 general elections, the Botswana Federation of Public Employees Organisations (BOFEPUSO) became directly engaged in BDP factional battles, 'de-campaigning' members of one faction. Hardly two years later, trade unions openly called for 'regime change' in Botswana during rallies they addressed during the national strike – rallies held in conjunction with opposition party members (*see* Ndlovu in this volume).

- Trade unions have also taken the route of reporting Botswana to the International Labour Organisation over disagreements with the government on labour matters.

- Civil society has used international avenues to apply pressure by reporting the government to a United Nations committee over perceived discriminatory practices concerning the non-recognition of the languages of minority ethnic groups (*see* Ndlovu in this volume).

These illustrations show a civil society that is growing in confidence, using various methods to engage the State, including direct confrontation, negotiation, partnerships and even international alliances. This turn of events in governance means that the State in Botswana has to find new ways of engaging with society. The oft-cited thesis of a 'weak' civil society in Botswana needs to be rethought.

REGIONAL AND WORLD PRESSURE

Botswana's democratic credentials have earned the country prestige in the international community out of proportion to its size, including a seat in the UN Security Council. However, signs are that this is changing.

- Botswana's perceived initial warmth towards hosting Africom (the United States Armed Forces Africa Command) led to threats of isolation, as has its willingness to arrest and hand over Sudanese president Omar al-Bashir to the ICC, in contrast with the position of the African Union (*see* Ndlovu in this volume).

- Botswana's willingness to criticise the Gadaffi regime in Libya, contrary to South Africa's position, led to allegations of displeasure in South Africa.

- While Botswana has been quick to criticise undemocratic regimes elsewhere, inconsistencies in foreign policy have caused criticism. For example, while Botswana has been critical of Robert Mugabe's Zimbabwe, it has cast a blind eye to the abuse of power by King Mswati of Swaziland, and to events in Malawi, where a recent public uprising led to security forces clashing with the demonstrators and the death of more than 19 people.

- Independence in both Namibia and South Africa led to a more rigorous analysis of Botswana. Theirs are more liberal, homegrown constitutions. South Africa's abolition of the death penalty contrasts sharply with Botswana's dispensation. The effect has been to bring into sharper focus Botswana's own system. A recent case in which a South African court of law refused to extradite murder suspects to Botswana, citing the possibility that they might be hanged under Botswana's capital punishment policy, offers an insight into the sharp differences between the two neighbours.

The tensions in foreign relations mean that Botswana's resolve to stay true to democratic credentials frequently faces external challenges. For instance, the tensions between South Africa and Botswana due to South Africa's refusal to extradite people accused of murder could compromise Botswana's judicial system. Similarly there are indicators that Botswana's position on Mugabe's Zimbabwe could be softening.[7] This rapprochement with the Zimbabwean government is not, however, because Zimbabwe has become any more democratic than it was. Apparently Botswana's wish to construct a railway and pipeline to Mozambique could be frustrated by Zimbabwe. Botswana has already softened its tone in dealing with Zimbabwe to the extent that it has been sending emissaries to Zimbabwe.[8] Where South Africa, a major trading partner and powerful neighbour is concerned, such tensions would be expected to lead to restrictions on Botswana's choices.

Botswana's long-held political stability is under renegotiation. This process is occurring in multiple arenas, including the courts of law, the media and in international forums such as the United Nations. At the centre of these challenges to the status quo is the need to carry out a broad-based process of democratic change in Botswana, towards the type of democracy that will enable citizens to participate more meaningfully in their country's affairs.

ENDNOTES

1 http://www.moibrahimfoundation.org/en/prizelaureates/the-ibrahim-prize/prize-laureates/the-ibrahim-prize-winner-2008-festus-gontebanye-mogae-1.html

2 http://www.moibrahimfoundation.org/en/section/the-ibrahim-index

3 http://www.transparency.org/policy_research/surveys_indices/cpi

4 *See*, for example, Kaboyakgosi (2003) on Botswana's 'cold' conflicts.

5 *Gomolemo Motswaledi v Botswana Democratic Party, Seretse Khama Ian Khama and Chairman*, Gaborone Central Branch.

6 Tshiamo Tabane. 2012. 'Constitutional reform could trigger political chaos – Pilane', *Sunday Standard*, 20 February 2012 [online]. Available: http://bit.ly/HO9LpQ.

7 *Sunday Standard* Reporter. 2012. 'BDF boss slams the West, praises Mugabe', *Sunday Standard*, 13 February 2012 [online]. Available: http://bit.ly/GQXOx8.

8 The Watchdog. 2012. 'Mugabe has Khama as one of his trophies' in *Sunday Standard*, 20 February 2012 [online]. Available: http://bit.ly/GPVYOh.

THE INDEX

100 QUESTIONS CONTEXTUALISING BOTSWANA'S DEMOCRACY

SECTION 1: PARTICIPATION AND DEMOCRACY

Though hailed as one of the oldest democracies in Africa, Botswana still needs to strengthen its democratic dispensation, specifically to ensure that it has an active citizenry. Education and engagement in political life are two ways in which that can be achieved. In this volume, Moatlhaping and Moletsane assess participation in terms of nationhood, participation and involvement, government legitimacy, citizenship obligations and duties, as well as tolerance. They observe that nationhood is challenged by the growing gap between citizens and the institutions that affect them, such as local and central government. Another challenge is with regard to non-Tswana-speakers, who feel the burden of being expected to assimilate into 'Tswanadom', something they fear may erode their ethnic identities. The authors also argue that Batswana are generally a tolerant nation: there have been no reported cases of xenophobia or discrimination against people because of their race or gender. However, the government is accused of intolerance towards sexual minorities, including its refusal to provide condoms in prisons, and its failure to give expatriate prisoners access to antiretrovirals. This section emphasises the need to strengthen existing oversight institutions.

SECTION 2: ELECTIONS AND DEMOCRACY

Gaontebale Mokgosi points out the connection between elections and democracy. He notes that although Botswana holds regular, free elections, it is equally important to ensure a fair electoral system. To this end, he raises several concerns with regard to the electoral process: the credibility and integrity of the Independent Electoral Commission (IEC), the lack of public funding of political parties, and floor-crossing. Mokgosi raises concern about the FPTP system, which, he claims, distorts the true picture of each party's popular support and does not allow for effective political representation. FPTP is derided by opposition parties as unfair and potentially undemocratic. Minorities are less likely to be elected under FPTP. Disabled persons and prisoners serving jail terms longer than six years are rarely given the chance to cast their vote. Mokgosi attributes the frequent political party splits to the lack of democracy within parties. On the other hand, the IEC is recognised for performing well in voter education, as many citizens have registered and voted in recent general elections. He notes that the IEC needs to address issues such as multiple voter registration and voter trafficking.

SECTION 3: ACCOUNTABILITY AND DEMOCRACY

Dr Botlhale argues that accountability (political and administrative) is a key tenet of democracy and necessary for good governance. Accountability cannot be discussed outside the concept of separation of powers among the executive, the judiciary and the legislature. While the Westminster system has worked well for Botswana so far, it gives the executive too many powers. Botlhale's concern is that the absence of structures enabling the legislature to call the executive to account limits the freedom of parliament. He argues that it is not enough that Members of Parliament only call the Cabinet to account during parliamentary question time. He notes that although the legislature can call the executive to account, this is a difficult and rare occurrence. Similarly, the devolution of powers to councils for easier management of public resources is only symbolic as they depend on central government funding, which limits them. With regard to public or administrative accountability, Botlhale argues that, although mechanisms for public consultation exist in the country, consultation as it is traditionally done through the *dikgotla* is marred by low attendance. However, the government has of late introduced *dipitso*, where stakeholders meet to contribute to policy and decision-making. It remains to be seen whether *dipitso* will prove effective or not.

SECTION 4: POLITICAL FREEDOMS AND DEMOCRACY

Thapelo Ndlovu argues that the dominance of the BDP has contributed to Botswana's political stability. He nevertheless notes that the BDP's competitive advantage is largely due to it enjoying preferential access to State media over the years. Ndlovu also acknowledges that the print media (both State and private) enjoy ease of registration and independence. However, he notes that although the Constitution of Botswana provides for the protection of civil and political freedoms, the extent to which people are able to protect themselves against discriminatory treatment by the State is limited. He notes the neglect of indigenous languages and cultures, giving the example of the appointment of members of the *Ntlo ya Dikgosi* (House of Chiefs). Several legal instruments and the absence of transparency are cited in this chapter as factors that compromise constitutional protection of the freedoms of expression, information and assembly. These include the immigration laws, the National Security Act (1986), the Media Practitioners Act (2009) and the Cinematograph Act (1972). Ndlovu points out that political parties are free to organise and that it is easy to form political parties in Botswana. He notes, though, that the call for electoral reforms has been rejected by the ruling party. Ndlovu questions the fairness of rules governing party discipline, which he suggests led to the BDP splitting, and hence the formation of the BMD. On access to information, he recognises the need for legislation supporting freedom of information. Ndlovu urges Botswana to review its Constitution so that it recognises second-generation rights and transparency laws, with the emphasis in the latter on the flow of information from the government to the people through an Act facilitating access to information.

SECTION 5: HUMAN DIGNITY AND DEMOCRACY

While Botswana is 'traditionally' regarded as the shining example of democracy in Africa, Melville and Mogwe argue that the country is party to only a few international human rights instruments, and that even these have not been domesticated. The main concern raised is the Constitution's silence on economic, social and cultural rights. The authors argue that, like many constitutions of the 1960s, Botswana's is focused more on political rights than economic, social and cultural rights. Despite the non-domestication of international instruments seeking to guarantee socio-economic rights, the State's commitment to these rights can be seen in the president's call for people-centred development in his 2010 State of the Nation address. However, the lack of recognition of socio-economic rights in the Constitution means there is no obligation on the government to provide basic socio-economic services to the population. The legal recognition of economic, social and cultural rights could go a long way towards guaranteeing human rights. Melville and Mogwe argue that such legal recognition does not, however, necessarily guarantee access. It is the presence of relevant policies, appropriate planning and legal protection that could guarantee human rights in Botswana.

The authors were asked to score each question between 1 and 10 using the following guide:

1–4   inadequate or falling short of the democratic ideal

5   stable but insufficient

6   stable and adequate

7   improving

8–10   excellent and as close to the democratic ideal as possible

SECTION ONE: PARTICIPATION AND DEMOCRACY

NATIONHOOD

1.	To what extent do leaders and citizens agree on the identity of the nation established by the territorial and legal State?	7
2.	To what extent do political leaders agree that democracy is the only appropriate form of making collective decisions for their nation?	9
3.	To what extent do political leaders and citizens resort to violence or illegal activity to settle political disputes?	8
4.	Do the majority of citizens agree that democracy is the only appropriate form of making collective decisions for their nation?	9

PARTICIPATION AND INVOLVEMENT

5.	To what extent do citizens participate in political life? Are citizens willing to participate in elections and become involved in other ways to influence government and hold it accountable?	5
6.	To what extent do citizens feel prepared and competent to take part in political life?	5
7.	To what extent do citizens feel that participation in political life can give them some ability to influence collective decisions?	4
8.	To what extent do citizens feel that the impact of their participation will be equal to other citizens?	4

GOVERNMENT LEGITIMACY

9.	To what extent do citizens feel that the government in general, and the present government in particular, has the right to make binding collective decisions?	8

CITIZENSHIP OBLIGATIONS AND DUTIES

10.	To what extent do citizens meet their legal obligations?	7

TOLERANCE

11.	To what extent do citizens tolerate ideas, peoples and practices with which they disagree?	7

SECTION 1 SCORE: 7

SECTION TWO: ELECTIONS AND DEMOCRACY

ELECTIONS

12.	Is appointment to legislative and executive office determined by popular election?	5
13.	To what extent are elections for government based on universal suffrage and secrecy of the ballot?	6
14.	Do all citizens believe that their vote is secret?	8
15.	To what extent do citizens believe that their electoral system reflects the will of the people? How much does the electoral system impact on representivity?	4

EQUAL VOTES		
16.	Do the votes of all electors carry equal weight?	4
17.	To what extent do citizens believe that they have equal influence?	4
OPEN COMPETITION		
18.	Is there equal opportunity for all groups who wish to organise and stand for office? Does social grouping make a difference?	4
19.	Are all political parties able to campaign free of threat?	8
20.	Are all citizens free to form opinions, voice them, persuade others and vote as they like, free of threat?	8
21.	How effective a range of choice does the electoral and party system allow the voters? Is there an open competition of ideas and policies?	4
ELECTION RULES		
22.	To what extent are voter registration procedures independent of control by government or individual political parties?	8
23.	To what extent are election procedures independent of control by government or individual political parties?	5
24.	To what extent are the advantages of incumbency regulated to prevent abuse in the conduct and contesting of elections?	4
25.	To what extent are voters able to register and to what extent have they registered to vote?	7
26.	Are election procedures free from abuse? And to what extent do citizens see election procedures as free from threat?	5
VOTER INFORMATION		
27.	How much information is conveyed to voters by the official election information system?	6
28.	How much information about political parties and candidates is conveyed by the news media? And how fairly is this done?	5
29.	How much access do political parties have to the media and how equitable is this?	5
30.	To what extent do the campaigns of political parties reach all sections of society?	4
31.	Do voters know enough about all political parties to be able to make an informed choice?	4
ELECTORAL PARTICIPATION		
32.	How extensively do citizens participate in elections?	8
33.	How are citizens able to influence the electoral process in ways other than the vote?	7
34.	To what extent is the management and control of the elections delegated to an independent body?	5
35.	Are there mechanisms for the review of the electoral system and are these open to citizen participation?	7

ELECTORAL OUTCOMES		
36.	Are the announced election results congruent with how the electorate actually cast their ballots?	3
37.	Do citizens believe that their vote makes a difference?	5
38.	Do security forces, the government and political parties accept the election results?	8
39.	Do citizens accept the election results?	8
40.	How closely do the composition of the legislatures and the selection of government reflect the election outcome?	3
41.	How far do the legislatures reflect the social composition of the electorate? To what extent are women represented in parliament?	3
FUNDING ELECTIONS		
42.	To what extent are private donations to political parties permitted and are they subject to regulation (such as transparency and limits), in order to prevent them from having a disproportionate impact on voter choice and electoral outcome?	3
43.	Is campaign finance – both income and expenditure – regulated?	4
	Are the political parties regulated by accepted procedures and non-partisan bodies? How extensive is the independent oversight of election expenditure?	5
44.	Is there public financing of political parties?	0

SECTION 2 SCORE: 5

SECTION THREE: ACCOUNTABILITY AND DEMOCRACY

EXECUTIVE ACCOUNTABILITY AND LEGISLATIVE OVERSIGHT		
45.	How far is the executive subject to the rule of law and transparent rules of government in the use of its powers? To what extent are all public officials subject to the rule of law and to transparent rules in the performance of their functions?	7
46.	How extensive and effective are the legislature's powers to scrutinise the executive, hold it to account, and initiate and scrutinise, as well as amend, legislation between elections? Is the legislature able to hold the executive to account for the implementation of legislation and policy?	5
47.	To what extent has legislative and executive power been devolved and what impact has this had on popular control?	4
PUBLIC PARTICIPATION AND ACCOUNTABILITY		
48.	How open, accessible, extensive and systematic are the procedures/mechanisms for public consultation and participation in legislation and policy-making? How equal is the access which interest groups/citizens have to influence the law-making process?	6

49.	How open, accessible, extensive and systematic are the procedures/mechanisms for public consultation and participation in executive policy? And how equal is the access which citizens have to influence executive policy?	6
50.	How far does government cooperate with relevant partners, associations and communities in forming and carrying out policies and how far are people able to participate in these processes?	6
LAW-MAKING AND THE BUDGET PROCESS		
51.	How extensive are the powers of legislative bodies, and how effective are they at legislating?	5
52.	How rigorous are the procedures for parliamentary approval, supervision of and input into the budget and public expenditure?	6
53.	How much say does the public have in the development of the budget? How well do parliamentary procedures allow the public to participate in decisions relating to resource allocation?	7
ACCESS TO INFORMATION		
54.	How independent and accessible is public information about government policies and actions and their effects? How comprehensive and effective is legislation giving citizens the right of access to government information?	4
ACCESSIBILITY AND INDEPENDENCE		
55.	How accessible are elected representatives to members of the public? What impact does the electoral and party system have on the way in which MPs represent people?	8
56.	How far are MPs protected from undue influence by outside interests? Are potential conflicts of interest regulated?	8
57.	How effective is the separation of public office, elected and unelected, from party advantage and the personal, business and family interests of office holders?	7
58.	How independent are the judiciary and the courts from the executive and from all kinds of interference?	8
59.	How effective and open to scrutiny is the control exercised by the legislature and the executive over civil servants?	7
60.	How far is the influence of powerful corporations and business interests over public policy kept in check, and how free are they from involvement in corruption?	8
61.	To what extent is the public service protected from corrupt practices? To what extent are public officials protected from undue influence by outside interests? Are potential conflicts of interest regulated?	7
62.	Are public servants who blow the whistle on corruption encouraged and protected? Are citizens who blow the whistle on corruption protected?	7

63.	To what extent can the government carry out its responsibilities in accordance with the wishes of the citizens, free of interference or constraint from political or economic forces outside of Botswana?	8
64.	How far is the government able to influence or control those things that are most important to the lives of its people, and how well is it organised, informed and resourced to do so?	9

SECTION 3 SCORE: 7

SECTION FOUR: POLITICAL FREEDOMS AND DEMOCRACY

CIVIL AND POLITICAL RIGHTS

65.	How free are all people from intimidation and fear, physical violation against their person, arbitrary arrest and detention?	5
66.	To what extent are people able to protect themselves against discriminatory treatment by the State?	4
67.	To what extent are people able to use the legal system to protect their person and property against the State?	6
68.	How effective is the protection of the freedoms of expression, information and assembly for all persons irrespective of their social grouping?	4

FREEDOM OF ASSOCIATION AND PARTICIPATION

69.	How secure is the freedom for all to practise their own religion, language and culture?	3
70.	To what extent do people feel free to associate with others in order to influence government? To what extent does government action encourage or discourage people to associate with others in order to influence government?	4
71.	To what extent do people organise themselves into associations in order to influence government and to what extent are the associations of civil society independent of government?	4
72.	How far do women participate in political and public life at all levels?	6
73.	How free from harassment and intimidation are individuals and groups working to protect human rights?	5

POLITICAL PARTIES

74.	How freely are political parties able to form, recruit members and engage with the public?	7
75.	How free are opposition or non-governing parties to organise within the legislature and outside of it?	6
76.	How fair and effective are the rules governing party discipline in the legislature and within the party?	6

77.	How far are parties effective membership organisations, and how far are members able to influence party policy? Are all individual members privy to sufficient information about their party, including details of private donors?	5
78.	To what extent are political parties able to aggregate the interest of all social groups?	5
MEDIA RIGHTS		
79.	To what extent does the legal system ensure that print and electronic media are free to print or say what they want about those in power in both government and the private sector?	5
80.	To what extent are people and organisations able to disseminate their views via print or electronic media?	7
81.	To what extent are the print and electronic media independent from government? How pluralistic is the ownership of print and electronic media?	5
82.	To what extent do citizens have equal access to adequate information, including news and other media?	2

Section 4 score: 5

SECTION FIVE: HUMAN DIGNITY AND DEMOCRACY

SOCIO-ECONOMIC RIGHTS PROTECTION		
83.	How far are economic and social rights, including equal access to work, guaranteed for all?	4
84.	How effectively are the basic necessities of life guaranteed, including a. Clean adequate and reasonably accessible water? b. Adequate food? c. Adequate housing and shelter? d. Adequate and unimpeded access to land?	4
HEALTH CARE		
85.	To what extent is the right to adequate health care protected in all spheres and stages of life? Is treatment available for illnesses such as HIV/Aids? Is access to treatment equitable?	6
EDUCATION		
86.	How extensive and inclusive is the right to education and training, including education on the rights and responsibilities of citizenship?	5
POVERTY		
87.	Are vulnerable groups such as children, people with disabilities and women adequately protected from poverty?	4
88.	How much impact on political participation does poverty have? How far are poor people able to participate in the wider Botswana society? To what extent are they excluded?	5

89.	To what extent is the State 'progressively realising' these social and economic rights in accordance with its constitutional obligations?	6
JOBS AND RIGHTS IN THE WORKPLACE		
90.	Is there equal opportunity for all, irrespective of ethnicity, in the workplace?	6
91.	How far are workers' rights to fair rates of pay, just and safe working conditions and effective representation guaranteed in law and practice?	4
92.	How far are wage levels and social security or other welfare benefits sufficient for people's needs, without discrimination (equally)?	2
DELIVERY OF SOCIAL AND ECONOMIC RIGHTS		
93.	Are public goods, for example water provision or local services such as waste collection, equally available to citizens and communities at similar levels of efficiency and competence?	4
94.	To what extent has privatisation had an impact on the adequate provision of public goods and services?	3
95.	To what extent do public-private partnerships or does privatisation facilitate or impede access to socio-economic rights, particularly for the poor?	3
96.	To what extent are private companies accountable for the delivery of socio-economic rights as a result of privatisation or public-private partnerships? To what extent is this accountability overseen by citizens or their representatives?	0
97.	To what extent do citizens feel they are receiving equal access to public resources regardless of their social grouping?	8
CORPORATE GOVERNANCE		
98.	How rigorous and transparent are the rules on corporate governance? And how effectively are corporations regulated in the public interest?	3
99.	To what extent are companies duty-bound to play a role in the realisation of socio-economic rights? And to what extent do they prioritise responsible social investment?	3
100.	Is the private sector meeting its new obligations, such as in relation to equity and empowerment responsibilities?	3
SECTION 5 SCORE: 4		
TOTAL SCORE: 6		

SECTION ONE

PARTICIPATION AND DEMOCRACY

BY SEGAMETSI OREEDITSE MOATLHAPING & KETLHOMILWE MOLETSANE

This section addresses participation and democracy in Botswana. In an effort to unravel the relationship between the two, it focuses on five elements: nationhood; participation and involvement; government legitimacy; citizenship obligations and duties; and tolerance.

Botswana has a long history of democracy and of indigenous forums that promote consultation. However, it is evident that work needs to be done to strengthen participatory democracy in the country. If 'participation' is defined in terms of the notion that 'through participation, the public are enabled to determine and control the allocation of development resources, not merely influence its direction' (Ambert 2000), then direct citizen participation is imperative for the consolidation of democracy and the establishment of sustainable development trajectories. It is vital for Botswana to promote and reinforce platforms that enhance citizens' active engagement with the understanding that the success or failure of the government is their responsibility. In this context, therefore, the emphasis on participation and democracy in this chapter relates to processes that promote bottom-up approaches to development. 'Participation' denotes the process of empowering citizens to develop intrinsic initiatives for self-reliant mobilisation, responsibility and control over how resources are used. In this way, citizens take collective action that improves their livelihoods and shun being passive recipients of resources allocated in a top-down fashion.

Botswana is, in traditional terms, a 'representative democracy'. As a result, the practice of public involvement in the democratisation processes over the years seems to have been based on a 'weak interpretation' of participation. According to De Beer (2000), a weak interpretation of participation equates public participation to simply involving people through co-option, placation, consultation and information, while not necessarily empowering them to participate in their own development meaningfully.

Notwithstanding this contention, Botswana's performance in governance and democracy is considered better than that of most of Africa. The country is politically and socially stable, with a predictable institutional, policy and legal environment. By all the governance indicators, Botswana has done exceptionally well in issues of political stability, government effectiveness, the rule of law and control of corruption. Since 2007, however, Botswana's standing on some principles of good governance has been declining or stagnant. For example, studies carried out by the World Bank Institute, World Economic Forum and International Budget Partnership reveal that some of Botswana's governance indicators are declining. Specifically, the Open Budget Index indicates that Botswana's performance in budget transparency dropped from 66% in 2007 to 51% in 2010 (BIDPA 2010). The country's weakening on this Index implies that citizens' strategic participation in decisions that affect their quality of life in Botswana is not fully open and dialogic. In addition, the Botswana Local Governance Barometer agrees that 'most community members have little knowledge and ability to comprehend technical budgeting issues' (BOCONGO et al. 2008:11) and, as such, feel marginalised in the budgeting process. In time, this might impact negatively on the capacity of Botswana to sustain good governance and democratic principles.

Additionally, the 2007 edition of The Economist Intelligence Unit's Index of Democracy scores Botswana very low in regard to the democratic indicators of political participation and political culture (Kekic 2007:3). This echoes a disturbing decline in Botswana's performance on 'voice and accountability', which, in terms of the World Bank's Worldwide Governance Indicators, measures the extent to which a country's citizens are able to participate in selecting their government and to enjoy freedom of expression, freedom of association and free media. According to this assessment, Botswana ranked number two in sub-Saharan Africa in 2003 and 2004, with 85%. The country dropped to number three in 2005 (65%), then stood at number seven in 2006 (50%), number six in 2007 (50%) and number five in 2008 (55%) (World Bank Institute 2003–2008). This decline might be due to a number of factors, including the limited capacity of citizens, particularly in illiterate and marginalised communities, to make their voices heard beyond the ballot box. According to the Vision 2016 Botswana Performance Report (Vision Council 2009), '[l]ack of Setswana language newspaper and community radio stations may limit information flow, particularly in rural areas', thus adversely affecting citizens' meaningful participation in public hearings, reviews of official documents, development of public policy and decision-making processes, as well as the Botswana political sphere generally.

Results of the the Mapping Local Democracy exercise by the Botswana Association of Local Authorities (BALA) substantiate the declines noted above. The research reveals that, while avenues for the promotion of participatory democracy exist, active participation in and attendance at such forums are often very poor (BALA 2007, 2009, 2010). This apparent apathy seems to be exacerbated by a decline in confidence in public institutions, including local authorities, which in turn results from slow and poor-quality service delivery by local authorities and central government. In addition, highly bureaucratic government processes and procedures constrain access to services. Further worsening the situation is a lack of transparency and limited accountability on the part of elected officials in addressing citizens' concerns, which detracts from people's interest in participating in the democratic and development processes.

The downward spiral in public confidence is worrying, because the factors underlying the decline are a sign that the State and local authorities are failing to carry out their core mandate, that of promoting democracy. In addition, the decline has implications for citizens' perceptions of democracy, particularly regarding the legitimacy of government, the rule of law, electoral participation and general participation in policy decisions that affect citizens' quality of life.

NATIONHOOD

1. To what extent do leaders and citizens agree on the identity of the nation established by the territorial and legal State? (7)

2. To what extent do political leaders agree that democracy is the only appropriate form of making collective decisions for their nation? (9)

3. To what extent do political leaders and citizens resort to violence or illegal activity to settle political disputes? (8)

4. Do the majority of citizens agree that democracy is the only appropriate form of making collective decisions for their nation? (9)

There is no simple definition of 'nationhood', but the notion can be equated to that of citizenship. For the purposes of this discussion, nationhood is a feature of an active, participatory democracy in which citizens enjoy their rights, exercise their duties, participate meaningfully and agree on a shared identity. In Botswana, 'nationhood' could be defined through the legal identity that distinguishes citizens from the expatriate community commonly referred to as 'residents or foreigners' (Preece & Mosweunyane 2003). In addition to the legal status of citizens in Botswana, the coat of arms, national flag and national anthem have been viewed as pre-eminent symbols and expressions of nationhood and patriotism (Presidential Task Group 1997).

Linking participation to nationhood raises fundamental and normative questions about the nature of democracy in Botswana, and about the national instruments and strategies for achieving and sustaining it. Benn, quoted in Preece & Mosweunyane (2003:6), defines 'citizenship' as 'involvement in social networks, in the groups, organisations that connect citizens with the life of their communities. Motivations to engage in other aspects of citizenship, such as attention to political and public issues, are reinforced through participation ... and engagement in civic and communal activities from good neighbourhood to charity-giving and to more formal socio-political activity'.

The critical challenge to address in Botswana is the growing gap between citizens and the institutions that affect their lives, particularly local authorities and central government institutions. Whereas Botswana has a history of consultation, tolerance, cooperation, collaborative responsibility, and political and social pluralism, there is a need to strengthen what has seemingly been a 'passive democracy' so that it becomes a 'participatory, responsive, transparent and accountable' democratic State at both local and national levels.

The people of Botswana have been officially identified, throughout the 45 years of democracy, as Batswana. The identity of Batswana, though implying homogeneity or mono-ethnic status, is based on the ethos of unity in diversity. Whereas the Tribal Territories Act of 1933 recognised the eight Tswana-speaking tribes of Bangwato, Bakwena, Bakgatla, Bangwaketse, Balete, Batawana, Barolong and Batlokwa, the 2005 amendment of sections 77, 78 and 79 of the Constitution had broader reference: though it focused on the composition of *Ntlo ya Dikgosi* (the representative house of traditional leaders), it recognised the existence and identities of other ethnic groups besides the eight previously identified as major tribes. Some scholars argue, however, that the 2005 constitutional amendment did not eliminate the potential for discrimination as it still allowed chiefs from the eight dominant 'Tswana' tribes to control the tribes led by 'sub-chiefs'. According to Cook and Sarkin (2008), this Tswana dominance has led to the continued marginalisation of existing minorities, to the point that minorities have little chance of making their presence felt in the Botswana social and political spheres.

In recent years, some groups in Botswana have contested nationhood. For example, the *Alternative Report Submitted to the Human Rights Committee on the International Covenant on Civil and Political Rights* by RETENG (the Multicultural Coalition of Botswana) argues that whereas all ethnic groups of citizens are identified as Batswana, not all of them – particularly not non-Tswana speakers – feel that their culture, customs and traditions, and therefore their identities, are recognised by the national territorial and legal State. The report claims that even simply referring to citizens of Botswana as 'Batswana' implies that non-Tswana are not recognised and are expected to assimilate themselves into 'Tswanadom', ultimately leading to the disappearance of their ethnic identities, culture and languages (RETENG 2007).

Despite these tensions, most leaders and citizens agree to identify as Batswana. Furthermore, there is consensus that national identity is grounded on the national development principles of *Botho*,[1] Democracy, Development, Self-Reliance and Unity, and that all citizens enjoy the fundamental rights and freedoms as spelt out by the Constitution of Botswana.

There continues to be broad accord in Botswana that democracy is the only truly appropriate form of government and remains an excellent system for collective decision-making and responsibility. No other system of government has ever been publicly advocated or endorsed by any leader or citizen. The majority of citizens, including Members of Parliament, have called for the strengthening or deepening and consolidation of democratic principles as highlighted in the national *Vision 2016* and Chapter 12 of *National Development Plan 10*. For instance, calls have been made by some political leaders and civil society for the transformation of the current representative democracy into a proportional representation system, for direct presidential elections, and for further political party funding to level the environment of political competitiveness and improve the accountability of the legislature and executive to citizens. These moves would, it is argued, strengthen the voice of ordinary citizens and enhance the government's accountability to them, thereby allowing them to influence government priorities and governance processes.

According to Lekorwe *et al*. (2001), the foundation of Botswana's democracy is embedded in the traditional *kgotla*[2] system. In agreeing with this contention, Moatlhaping (2007:11) notes: 'In today's era, the *kgotla* is a central consultative mechanism through which public policies are explained and through the *kgotla* the populace in turn pronounce on issues, ideas and views.' Institutions such as the Organisation of Economic Cooperation and Development (OECD) (OECD 2010) argue that Botswana developed proto-democratic institutions before British rule. The chiefs held the position of first among equals, rather than a hierarchical position. In this regard, the indigenous or traditional governance system allows for the growth of a democratic system in Botswana. Critics of the Botswana indigenous form of governance (the *kgotla* system and the customary courts), such as former president Festus Mogae and columnist Dan Moabi, have argued that the system tends to be undemocratic and has no place in modern-day Botswana. They further contend that, although this traditional governance system provides 'space' and forums for public consultation, tribal belonging and free access to justice, the custodians of the *kgotla* – that is, the chiefs or *dikgosi* – are not elected, but simply inherit the leadership positions, and therefore can never be true representatives of the community (Moabi 2006).

The recent split in the ruling BDP, with the subsequent formation of the Botswana Movement for Democracy (BMD), was perceived by many to be a result of the ruling party's failure to comply consistently with democratic principles. In addition, some have argued that the non-existence of internal party democracy in 'strong' opposition parties such as the BCP (with the party president not directly elected by party members) is equally undemocratic. While most citizens agree that democracy is the best system of government for Botswana, there is evidence of significant concern over floor-crossing by elected officials. Reasons advanced for this include the fact that once elected, political leaders tend to represent their own interests at the expense of citizens' needs and priorities, and as a result compromise the ability of citizens to hold them accountable.

However, apart from the highly criticised intra-party violence in the Botswana National Front (BNF) in 1998, which led to the formation of the BCP, neither political leaders nor citizens of Botswana have ever used political violence or illegal activities to settle disputes. In general, one may conclude that these leaders and citizens have demonstrated improved confidence in the democratic system over the past four decades. It can further be concluded that a democratic culture, characterised by a multi-party system, freedom of association and a drive for the consolidation of democracy, has been firmly established.

Participation and Involvement

5. To what extent do citizens participate in political life? Are citizens
    willing to participate in elections and become involved in other ways
    to influence government and hold it accountable?   (5)

6. To what extent do citizens feel prepared and competent to take part in
    political life?   (5)

7. To what extent do citizens feel that participation in political life can give
    them some ability to influence collective decisions?   (4)

8. To what extent do citizens feel that the impact of their participation will
    be equal to other citizens?   (4)

Both the national *Vision 2016* and the *National Development Plan 10* have key result areas aimed at ensuring that, by 2016, Botswana's democracy is strengthened. For example, *Vision 2016* states:

> Botswana's democratic process will be deepened through full involvement and meaningful contribution to social, economic, political, entrepreneurial, spiritual and cultural development by all citizens that is informed by a culture of transparency, accountability and consultation … emphasising the accountability of all citizens from the State President down to the community leaders for their actions and decisions (Presidential Task Group 1997:74).

In line with the above, the Independent Electoral Commission (IEC), Botswana National Youth Council, Botswana Association of Local Authorities (BALA) and Emang Basadi (a women's development organisation) have, over the years, undertaken voter education initiatives in an effort to encourage active participation by citizens in political life. Government institutions alike utilise public places such as *kgotla*, the High Level Consultative Council (HLCC) meetings, and recently the *dipitso* (singular *pitso* – named after the traditional tribal forums normally called by the chief to discuss community issues) for the promotion of citizen engagement. These platforms are predominantly used to discuss district and urban development plans, and other national policy and development issues. However, most community members attending these forums do not have the capacity to fully comprehend and engage in meaningful discussion of all the decisions that affect their lives (BALA 2009). Generally, and despite efforts by the IEC and civil society institutions to educate the public on politics and the impact on socio-economic development, there is still a low level of active participation in political life on the part of citizens, particularly marginalised groups such as Basarwa, youth, people with disabilities and women.

Until 1994, the representation of women in parliament and local government was low. Notwithstanding the improvement in representation recorded in 1994, a significant decline was noted in 2004. The literature shows that the representation of women in the executive (Cabinet) was 18% in 2004, but declined to 11% in 2009 (IEC 2009).

While interest in politics is growing among citizens of Botswana in general, there also seem to be worrying signs of political indifference among young people and people with disabilities, specifically because these groups doubt the impact of their views and concerns on decision-making processes (Ntsabane & Ntau 2000).

The IEC has continued to record high levels of voter apathy in Botswana since 2002. There is little consensus on the reasons for this, though suggestions include illiteracy, inadequate voter and civic education (by political parties and others), socio-economic factors, the unaccountability of politicians and low confidence in the government. Despite this worrying trend, voting in national and primary elections remains the primary means with which the majority of Batswana hold their politicians accountable.

While there are opportunities for citizens to attend sessions of parliament and council meetings, public participation remains limited for reasons including time constraints, lack of resources to facilitate attendance, limited access to contextually effective information, and the fact that some technical debates are not readily comprehensible to ordinary citizens. As a result, there is generally low political participation outside the national elections (Maundeni 2005).

A significant number of Batswana are interested in public affairs and discuss politics 'frequently' on public and private radio stations, as well as in the print media (Cook & Sarkin 2008). Most citizens contend that a lack of access to information and a general lack of transparency on the part of public institutions limit full participation in the development processes, including political life. This is compounded by the non-existence of effective forums for holding public servants and elected officials directly to account, apart from elections.

The definition of 'democracy' in Botswana seems to be skewed towards the consistent holding of national elections, and the mechanistic establishment of infrastructure and bureaucratic processes and procedures at the expense of a 'strategic' approach to democratic involvement: open and transparent, consensual and responsive, equitable and inclusive, participatory, progressive and accountable facilitative democratic governance, all aimed at empowered citizenship. As a result, the effective participation and engagement of citizens in building and sustaining democracy remains the weakest link.

GOVERNMENT LEGITIMACY

9. To what extent do citizens feel that the government in general, and the present government in particular, has the right to make binding collective decisions? (8)

'Government legitimacy' can be defined as a status conferred by the people on a government's officials, Acts and institutions through their belief that the government's actions are an appropriate use of power by a legally constituted governmental authority following correct decisions on making policies. The OECD (2010:12) argues that the definition of government legitimacy can be based on four focus areas:

• Input or process legitimacy, which is tied to agreed rules of procedure

- Output or performance legitimacy, defined in relation to the effectiveness and quality of public goods and services (with security playing a central role in fragile situations)

- Shared beliefs, including a sense of political community, and beliefs shaped by religion, traditions and 'charismatic'leaders, and

- International legitimacy, i.e. recognition of the State's external sovereignty and legitimacy.

On one hand, international institutions that rank governance, including the Mo Ibrahim Foundation, Transparency International, the United Nations Economic Commission for Africa and the locally based Botswana Institute for Development Policy Analysis (BIDPA), rate Botswana highly on good governance, compared to most other African countries. Specifically on 'government effectiveness', an indicator that measures the quality of public services, the quality of the civil service and its degree of independence from political pressures, the quality of policy formulation and implementation, and the credibility of the government's commitment to such policies (World Bank Institute 2006), Botswana was placed at number 11 in the world and number three in sub-Saharan Africa (World Bank 2011). One must treat certain conclusions on the perception on Botswana's performance with caution, however, because these indicators are generated from, and often represent, the views of high-ranking government officials, members of the business community, technocrats and academics, but seldom include the views of ordinary citizens.

The *National Vision 2016 Household Opinion Survey* (Vision Council 2010a) reveals moderate citizen satisfaction (at 54%) with the way in which the government is running the country. The majority of citizens seem supportive of how the government is handling the economy and its diversification, improving access to and the quality of services, developing infrastructure, addressing poverty eradication and reducing unemployment.

Over the years Botswana has done well in terms of maintaining the rule of law and improving confidence in the judiciary. There is general consensus that the judiciary is independent of influence from the executive. The recent introduction of small claims and industrial courts in Botswana is said to have somewhat improved access to justice. Table 1.1 sets out the results of a survey by the Vision Council (2010a) that asked citizens about their confidence in the judicial system.

Table 1.1: Confidence in judicial organisations				
Type of court	Response in %			
	High	Low	None	Don't know
Customary	51	42	4	3
Magistrate	61	28	7	4
High Court	63	22	9	6
High Court of Appeal	55	21	15	9
Small claims	39	25	21	15
Industrial	40	32	17	11
Source: Vision Council 2010a.				

On the other hand, some citizens, particularly in the political sphere, have been critical of government stances on issues such as the Intelligence Bill of 2007 and the subsequent Intelligence Act, some seeing it as a sign of the erosion of democracy. Additionally, they have questioned the credibility and ability of oversight institutions such as parliament (Vision Council 2010a:37).

There have also been calls for local government to be strengthened by decentralising socio-political decision-making and management to local authorities. Proponents of local government democracy argue that this is the level of democracy that is closest to the people, and allows citizens to engage actively and directly in affairs that immediately affect their livelihoods (BALA 2009).

Overall it seems Botswana is doing well in the area of government legitimacy. More needs to be done, however, to strengthen the oversight institutions at both national and local government levels.

Citizenship obligations and duties

10. To what extent do citizens meet their legal obligations? (7)

In line with the democratic principle of the rule of law, the citizens of Botswana, and even government institutions, broadly speaking, comply with their legal obligations. There is generally law and order in the country, and the rules and procedures by which the State enforces its laws are public and explicit – not secret, arbitrary or subject to political manipulation. The efforts to make laws public and explicit seem, however, limited to the rule of law.

Additionally, the Heritage Foundation (2009) noted that Botswana had a functioning taxation system with the lowest tax rates in Southern Africa. As a result, tax revenue in 2008 accounted for 35.2% of the gross domestic product. This is an indication that taxable individuals do meet their obligation to pay tax, thus participating in national economic development.

The growing incidence of crimes such as housebreaking, rape, armed robbery, 'passion killings' and suicide, as well as road accidents, across Botswana may pose challenges of citizenship and compliance with legal obligations. There is a need to develop strategic initiatives that deter citizens from breaking the law and encourage them to meet their legal obligations, so that they can, at the same time, enjoy their rights and exercise their responsibilities.

Tolerance

11. To what extent do citizens tolerate ideas, peoples and practices with which they disagree? (7)

Batswana are generally a tolerant nation. There have been no registered cases of xenophobia or discrimination against people because of their race or gender. However, the government of Botswana has recently been accused of intolerance towards minorities (Cook & Sarkin 2008). The Vision Council (2010a) survey results substantiate the deep sense of tolerance among citizens. The respondents were asked to rate their levels of tolerance of religious, gender, age and racial differences.

Table 1.2: Tolerance of diverse groups in communities					
Attribute	Response in %				
	Definitely agree	Tend to agree	Disagree	Tend to disagree	Don't know
Religion	56	20	19	3	1
Gender	58	24	15	2	1
Age	53	26	19	2	1
Race	46	21	25	6	3
Source: Vision Council 2010a..					

CONCLUSION

In the 45 years of Botswana's independence, the country has made strides in maintaining solidarity and unity among its citizens. The literature shows that many Batswana embrace a significantly strong sense of national identity as enshrined in the Constitution and Citizenship Act.

It is evident that the majority of Batswana agree that democracy is a good system and an appropriate form of governance, hence the identified need for citizens to be involved in the performance of national and local public duties. Whereas participation in national elections is evident, though perceptibly declining, there is limited participation in political life outside elections. This shows that stakeholders, government, civil society and other non-State actors all need to engage in civic education. It is reasonable to expect that strategic civic education would increase the capacity of citizens to participate in the democratisation of Botswana.

Similarly, when people know their rights and responsibilities, they will demand, in turn, high-quality services and have the ability to hold government accountable. Strengthened accountability on the part of the government is expected, in turn, to strengthen Botswana's democracy. Confidence in the legitimacy of government, though perceived to be in a healthy state, nevertheless appears to require attention, particularly in terms of oversight institutions and the equitable distribution of resources and service provision. Failure to address issues of equity could threaten citizens' willingness to comply with the rule of law.

ENDNOTES

1 *Botho* is a Setswana word that means 'humaneness'. An unnamed politician quoted in Preece and Mosweunyane (2003:9) defines *botho* as 'having qualities [associated with] character – a well rounded person, compassion, good neighbourliness, extending courtesy to others, doing unto others what you would have done unto you'.

2 A *kgotla* is a forum where community consultations take place (plural: *dikgotla*). It is also a court where civilian and criminal cases brought before the *kgosi* (traditional leader) are adjudicated (Schapera 1970:67–68)

SECTION TWO

ELECTIONS AND DEMOCRACY[1]

BY GAONTEBALE MOKGOSI

In any democracy, elections are mechanisms through which citizens participate directly in the political process and elect their fellow citizens into office for restricted periods of time (Democracy Research Project 2002:76). While such fair political competition is the hallmark of liberal democratic practice, democracy is not only about holding free and fair elections, but also about having a fair electoral system in place. When Botswana gained independence, elections were conducted by the Office of the President under the direction of the permanent secretary to the president. This arrangement caused complaints among opposition parties because the permanent secretary was directly responsible to the president. To address this concern, the Constitution was amended to provide, in S66(1), for a Supervisor of Elections to take overall charge of administering elections in the country. But this reform was not enough for the opposition parties, which continued to complain, especially because S66(2) of the Constitution stipulated: 'The Supervisor of Elections shall be appointed by the president.' Moreover, the presidential appointment of the Supervisor of Elections was not subject to approval by any independent body or authority. This arrangement left the independence of that office very much in doubt and tainted the fairness of the electoral process.

In an effort to nurture and sustain the democratic process, the Botswana government established the Independent Electoral Commission (IEC) in 1997 with the mandate to manage the electoral process and provide civic education. Since its establishment, Botswana's IEC has successfully conducted three national elections, numerous by-elections and a national referendum. The national elections in 1999, 2004, and 2009 were declared peaceful and free of violence. This assessment was endorsed by other stakeholders, such as election observers, who commended the commission for delivering credible elections.

Although the IEC is an oversight institution that manages national elections, its credibility and the integrity of the electoral process remain a political issue. There is a strong perception that the IEC is not sufficiently autonomous, for a number of reasons: the IEC Secretary is appointed by the Head of State and not by the IEC. Moreover, the IEC does not issue a writ of elections; the president does. This has become an issue of public debate because the president and the Minister of Local Government are interested parties.

Upon its political independence in 1965, Botswana adopted the British Westminster system of governance, including its plurality-majority electoral system. Through this system, the country is divided into constituencies, each of which elects one representative to parliament, and the winner of an election secures a victory on the basis of a simple plurality of votes. That is why the system is also often referred to as the first-past-the-post (FPTP) or winner-take-all system. It is this feature of the FPTP system that results in legislative bodies that do not reflect the will of the people. The system dilutes the most potent weapon that the electorate has – their vote (Molomo 2005:40).

Another important thing about Botswana's elections is the fact that there is no public funding of political parties. Political candidates have argued that this guarantees inequalities among contesting political parties and limits the scope of democracy. The funding of political parties is of critical importance in ensuring the necessary competition in the electoral process as it levels the political playing field for parties and candidates.

This section will focus on the Botswana electoral system, its components and processes in order to assess the state of this important democratic institution. It will also make a case for reform of the electoral system to include proportional representation, legislation and/or regulation relating to public party funding, fixed dates for general elections, mobile voting stations for special voters, the right of employees to be released on election day and the total independence of the IEC.

ELECTIONS

12. Is appointment to legislative and executive office determined by popular election? (5)

13. To what extent are elections for government based on universal suffrage and secrecy of the ballot? (6)

Botswana has been widely regarded as a model democracy because its conduct of elections is deemed generally satisfactory. Botswana holds elections every five years, in accordance with two legal instruments: the Constitution of Botswana and the Electoral Act (1968).

Botswana has no direct elections to executive office. The party with the most seats in the legislature chooses the president of the country. The president, in turn, appoints the Cabinet and can accept or reject the advice of the Cabinet (Maundeni 2008:30). In the interests of strengthening Botswana's democracy, the Constitution ought to be amended to provide for the election of the president by popular vote.

The Constitution and the Electoral Act (1968) guarantee all citizens of 18 years and older the right to vote in regular popular elections for any legislature. However, the electoral law in Botswana does not provide for voters with special needs, such as the aged and infirm or those in hospitals. They are expected to go to polling stations, a requirement which effectively disenfranchises them. The other shortcoming of the Electoral Act is that it does not give employees the right to time off work for voting. Such a predicament has denied employees in the private sector their full right to vote.

Appropriate changes to the Electoral Act are needed to address these shortcomings. The special vote categories should include registered persons who are unable to reach their voting stations on election day because they are temporarily absent on holiday or business, for example. Benchmarking on special votes can be done with South Africa's Electoral Commission and the right to time off from work for voting with the Malawi Electoral Commission.

14. Do all citizens believe that their vote is secret? (8)

15. To what extent do citizens believe that their electoral system reflects the will of the people? How much does the electoral system impact on representivity? (4)

S65A of the Constitution of Botswana gives the IEC the responsibility to ensure that elections are conducted efficiently, properly, freely and fairly (IEC 2010b:26). Botswana voting procedures allow only one voter at a time into the polling room. Only once the voter has cast his/her ballots for both national and local elections is the next voter allowed into the polling room. In order to ensure the integrity of elections, party agents are present to monitor the voting and counting processes.

Botswana's FPTP electoral system does not provide for effective political representation. Council and parliamentary electoral outcomes do not reflect the broad interests represented in society, and the winner-take-all system excludes some interests in society. A FPTP system aggravates an uneven political playing field, generously rewarding the ruling party with parliamentary seats even when its popular vote is decreasing. Since independence this has given the Botswana Democratic Party (BDP) a disproportional number of seats compared to its popular vote: in 2009, the party's 53% of the popular vote gave it 78% of the seats (45 out of the total of 57).

The failure of FPTP systems to produce representative governments is increasingly being criticised (IEC 2010b:26). Apart from the fact that women, young people and minorities are less likely to be elected to the legislature under a FPTP system, it exaggerates the phenomenon of 'regional fiefdoms', where one party wins all the seats in an area. If a party has strong support in a particular part of the country and thus wins a plurality of votes, it will gain all, or nearly all, of the legislature seats for that area. A FPTP system also encourages candidates to develop personal attachments to wards and constituencies, to the extent that when they lose primary elections, they defect to opposing parties or stand as independent candidates (Molomo 2005:38). According to the 2002 voter apathy report, 72.5% of voters indicated that all political parties should be represented in parliament (Democracy Research Project 2002:76). Botswana therefore needs to hold a popular dialogue on the electoral system in a democratic spirit, with the aim of fostering inclusive political participation and fairer competition.

Table 2.1 sets out voter support per party in the parliamentary elections under the FTPT system. The second part of the table demonstrates how the results would have differed under proportional representation.

Table 2.1: Party support in parliamentary elections 1965–2009										
Number of seats: first past the post										
Party	1965	1969	1974	1979	1984	1989	1994	1999	2004	2009
BDP	28	24	27	29	28	31	27	33	44	45
BNF	-	3	2	2	5	3	13	6	12	6
BIP/IFP	0	1	1	0	0	0	0	-	-	-
BPU	0	0	0	0	0	0	-	-	-	-
BPP	3	3	2	1	1	0	0	-	-	-
BCP	-	-	-	-	-	-	-	1	1	4
BAM	-	-	-	-	-	-	0	0	0	1
NDF	-	-	-	-	-	-	-	-	0	-
MELS	-	-	-	-	-	-	0	0	0	0
Independent	-	-	-	-	-	-	-	-	-	1
Total seats										57
Number of seats: proportional representation										
BDP	25	21	25	24	23	22	22	23	30	30
BNF	-	4	4	4	7	9	15	10	15	13
BIP/IFP	2	2	1	2	1	1	1	-	-	11
BPU	0	0	0	0	0	0	-	-	-	-
BPP	4	4	2	2	2	2	2	-	-	1
BCP	-	-	-	-	-	-	-	5	10	
BAM	-	-	-	-	-	-	0	2	2	1
NDF	-	-	-	-	-	-	-	-	0	-
MELS	-	-	-	-	-	-	0	0	0	0
Independent	-	-	-	-	-	-	-	-	-	1
Total seats										57

The opposition parties and civil society organisations continue to argue against the FPTP system, saying it distorts the truth about each party's popular support. The electoral system in its present state encourages a dominant party system and exaggerates the weaknesses of opposition parties (Molomo 2005:40). It exhibits inbuilt tendencies of authoritarianism rather than rule by consensus (Molomo 2005:40).

The fact that the current system works against, rather than for, an accurate representation of all voices suggests the need to review the FPTP system in favour of a more representative and democratic one.

EQUAL VOTES

16. Do the votes of all electors carry equal weight?   (4)

17. To what extent do citizens believe that they have equal influence?   (4)

The leaders of the ruling BDP argue in favour of the Westminster simple-majority system, or FPTP system, adopted at independence, saying it is simple to implement and ensures a close connection between voters and their representatives, thus promoting geographical accountability (IEC 2010b:26). Also, they argue, the fact that Botswana has never experienced political turmoil during elections shows that the system works well for the country. But the opposition's view is that the BDP wants the FPTP system to continue because it has the most to lose from any changes to the system. Opposition representatives say the FPTP system is unfair and potentially undemocratic, in that the number of seats won by the BDP is disproportionate to its popularity with the public: a party that wins 10% of the votes should win approximately 10% of the legislative seats. In the 2009 national elections, the BDP obtained 53% of the popular vote, but this translated into 78% of parliamentary seats, or 45 out of the total of 57. Under proportional representation it would have won 30 seats and the opposition 27 (IEC 2010b:26).

Floor-crossing is a feature of the FPTP system which allows elected representatives defecting from one political party to another to retain their seats in the legislature or council, despite the fact that those seats were won on behalf of their former party. However, the movement of elected representatives, although allowed by the Constitution and the electoral system, tends to destabilise the elective body and undermine the legitimacy and accountability of Members of Parliament (MPs) and councillors. Above all, it weakens the political value of representative democracy. Furthermore, floor-crossing happens without the consent of the electorate. Because the MPs or councillors are not compelled to seek a new mandate after crossing the floor, some observers see floor-crossing as unfair and a betrayal of voters. This situation undermines the vertical accountability of elected representatives to the electorate.

The compound effect of power struggles and the lack of internal democracy within political parties further explains the splits and floor-crossing. Both ruling and opposition parties experience internal discord and disharmony marked by conflict and factionalism, and these tend to cause splits. Some observers have argued that the quality of democracy within certain major political parties in Botswana is suspect, and that most parties do not follow their constitutions – or, where they do, the constitutions contain undemocratic provisions such as those that centralise decision-making powers in the party's leadership (IEC 2010b:41). Party leaders are said to be manipulating primary elections to sideline candidates who are deemed controversial. As a result, some party activists have resigned from their parties, while others have been expelled for alleged 'indiscipline' and 'disloyalty' to the party (Democracy Research Project 2002:83).

What is needed to address floor-crossing in Botswana is a constitutional provision for the recall of constituency or ward MPs or councillors by their electorate, in cases where the voters feel that representatives are no longer living up to the expectations of their constituents.

OPEN COMPETITION

18. Is there equal opportunity for all groups who wish to organise and stand for office? Does social grouping make a difference? (4)

The Constitution of Botswana protects every citizen's freedom of expression. It states:

> no person shall be hindered in the enjoyment of his freedom of expression, that is to say, freedom to hold opinions without interference, ... freedom to communicate ideas and information without interference ... and freedom from interference with his correspondence (ROB 1997:S12(1)).

In essence, the legal framework exists to promote proper conduct by all stakeholders and actors in the electoral process. However, electoral campaigns in Botswana are beset by many imbalances in terms of equity and fairness. The coverage of ruling party rallies on government radio and television, and in the government-owned *Daily News* newspaper, which is supplied free nationwide, has always been disproportionate (IEC 2010b:43). This bias remains a bone of contention in elections. The Department of Broadcasting Services, for instance, gives more coverage to the ruling party than the opposition during election campaigns. Even the National Broadcasting Board demanded in 2009 that the State media follow its code; however, the department ignored this ruling (IEC 2010b:43).

Another issue of concern related to electoral campaigning is the State funding of political parties. The opposition has, over the years, agitated for parties and candidates to receive public financing so as to be able to campaign effectively. The ruling BDP opposes such funding, however, saying that State resources should rather be spent on development (IEC 2010b). The opposition, in turn, regards the BDP position as insensitive and unfair, pointing out that, as the ruling party, its members often benefit from access to State resources such as subsidised travel across the country, under the pretext of executing government duties.

The lack of State funding of political parties has created an uneven political playing field for aspiring candidates, with a particularly negative impact on opposition parties, young people and women candidates. Introducing State funding would guarantee political equality and participation, and would give parties a certain level of political visibility and effective competition in the political arena. Botswana therefore needs to consider introducing a law on party funding.

19. Are all political parties able to campaign free of threat?   (8)

20. Are all citizens free to form opinions, voice them, persuade others
    and vote as they like, free of threat?   (8)

21. How effective a range of choice does the electoral and party system
    allow the voters? Is there an open competition of ideas and policies? (4)

Botswana provides adequate measures for fostering proper conduct by all stakeholders and actors in the electoral processes. The Code of Conduct for Political Parties covers a broad spectrum of 'dos and don'ts', such as the prohibition of any form of intimidation, the carrying of weapons, hate speech, disfigurement of the environment, preventing any person from attending the meeting of another party and disrupting other parties' rallies. Party leaders must enforce the code, and those who violate it have to be reported to the party liaison committee, the IEC Secretary or the police. The country also has a well-defined media regulatory framework that is contained in the Code of Conduct for Broadcasters as set out in the Broadcasting Act (1998). The code encourages equitable and professional treatment of political parties and independent candidates by the media during elections.

These provisions have generally been adhered to, despite the fact that they are guidelines and have no legal force. However, incidents of biased reporting in favour of the BDP and inequitable media access by ruling party candidates, especially to the public media, surfaced during the 2009 elections. These included opposition parties' complaints that both the president and his deputy enjoyed unfettered access to the public media, which gave them an unfair advantage over other candidates (IEC 2010b:45).

In order to enhance the legal enforceability of these codes of conduct, they need to be incorporated into electoral law and supported by a solid sanctions regime.

Botswana's FPTP system does not guarantee equal and fair election processes. In this system a large number of votes are wasted by being cast for losing candidates in winner-take-all contests. This can be particularly dangerous in the context of regional fiefdoms, because minority party supporters in a region may begin to feel that they have no realistic hope of ever getting a candidate of their choice elected. The system excludes women from the legislature: the fact that men were the first to play a leading role in Botswana's political arena has given them an economic advantage over women. The poor economic background of most women in Botswana makes it difficult for them to succeed in parliament or local councils under the FPTP system. The 'most broadly acceptable candidate' syndrome also impairs the ability of women to be elected to legislative office, because they are less likely to be selected as candidates by male-dominated party structures.

While the electoral environment allows for open and free competition by interested parties, the lack of public funding for political parties prevents many from holding effective election campaigns. The absence of a law to regulate private party funding worsens the situation and has created a big wealth gap between the ruling BDP and the opposition parties.

ELECTION RULES

22. To what extent are voter registration procedures independent of control by government or individual political parties?   (8)

23. To what extent are election procedures independent of control by government or individual political parties?   (5)

24. To what extent are the advantages of incumbency regulated to prevent abuse in the conduct and contesting of elections?   (4)

The IEC is mandated to manage the electoral process and the conduct of elections for the National Assembly and local government, and to provide civic and voter education to increase participation by the electorate (IEC 2010b:1).

As the name states, the IEC is supposed to be an independent body and several mechanisms have been put in place to ensure its independence. In terms of the Constitution (ROB 1997:S65A), the IEC shall consist of:

- a Chairman who shall be a judge of the High Court appointed by the Judicial Service Commission

- a legal practitioner appointed by the Judicial Service Commission

- five other persons who are fit, proper and impartial, appointed by the Judicial Service Commission from a list of persons recommended by the All Party Conference.

The Judicial Service Commission (JSC) is an independent body that recommends the appointment of judicial officers in the country (Lekorwe & Tshosa 2005:53).

All other administrative and operational provisions for elections in Botswana are contained in a separate Act of Parliament, the Electoral Act. The Act stipulates the mechanisms and procedures for voter registration, the conduct of polls, the regulation of candidates' election expenses, corrupt and illegal practices, and petitions, among other things.

The legal framework for elections in Botswana is also informed by regional instruments governing elections of the Southern African Development Community (SADC), such as the Principles for Electoral Management, Monitoring and Observation in the SADC Region, and the SADC Principles and Guidelines for Democratic Elections, to which Botswana is a signatory. But it is surprising that Botswana has neither signed nor ratified the African Charter on Democracy, Elections and Governance.

There are doubts among electoral stakeholders about whether the IEC is sufficiently autonomous. These are given credence by the fact that the Constitution provides for the IEC Secretary to be appointed by the president and not by the commission itself. Even the appointment of the chairman of the commission is contentious because, as a judge of the High Court, he is appointed by the president of Botswana. What seems to further limit the IEC's independence is the fact that it receives funds and accounts for them in the same way as a government department (IEC 2010b:29). The IEC does not have the power to hire and fire its staff, and it relies on seconded civil servants to perform its work. There is also a public perception that the IEC's dependence on government authorities for transport compromises its independence. The public also feel that the IEC budget restrains its mandate and capacity to reach out to society at large in its activities and administrative functions.

The authority to call elections rests with the president and the Minister of Local Government. Neither the country's Constitution nor the Electoral Act provides for the president to consult any person or office before he or she determines the date.

The non-regulation of external funding tarnishes the electoral process in that the ruling party, by virtue of its incumbency, attracts significant cash donations from local and international donors, while smaller political parties struggle for wider outreach to the electorate. Despite these challenges there is growing public confidence in the IEC and its capacity to deliver credible elections. Botswana must consider ratifying the African Charter on Democracy, Elections and Governance to enhance its democratic standing. A seminar is also needed to assess how well Botswana's IEC has performed in satisfying the Principles and Guidelines on the Independence of Election Management Bodies in the SADC Region, drawn up by the SADC's Electoral Commissions Forum and adopted by Botswana.

25. To what extent are voters able to register and to what extent have they registered to vote? (7)

26. Are election procedures free from abuse? And to what extent do citizens see election procedures as free from threat? (5)

Voters register in Botswana in three different ways: general registration, supplementary registration and continuous registration. In accordance with S5 of the Electoral Act, 2 228 local polling stations and 26 external polling stations were established with the help of party liaison committees, local authorities and Botswana embassies. For each registration period, 4 576 registration officers were recruited from among school learners and teachers, and 133 supervisors were engaged to oversee the work of the registration officers (IEC 2010b:3).

In the run-up to the 2009 elections, the IEC conducted a successful voter registration exercise, both inside and outside the country, recording 723 617 registrations, or about 68% of the eligible population. Of the total, 404 283 were female and 321 534 male. First-time voters (those between the ages of 18 and 29) numbered 240 055, constituting over 30% of those registered, which indicates an unprecedented interest in elections among Botswana's young people (IEC 2010b:71). The statistics represent an increase relative to previous elections.

The high registration figures were largely attributed to the sustained voter education campaigns undertaken by the IEC and some civil society groups, including the media. In 2007, the IEC conducted six regional workshops to engage young people in dialogue about their lack of participation in the electoral process. The recommendations from these workshops were shared with other stakeholders and used to map out strategies, including education with roadshows to address voter apathy, especially among eligible young people (IEC 2010b:2)

The IEC also addressed prospective candidates for the 2009 general elections and their campaign managers to update them on its state of preparedness for the elections, and to acquaint them with the legal requirements on the nomination of candidates, the polling and counting of votes, and other critical electoral processes.

However, some parties, electoral observers and potential voters had complaints about the registration process (IEC 2010b:40). Stakeholders expressed concern about multiple voter registration and voter trafficking in certain polling districts, especially in the urban areas (IEC 2010b:40). Multiple registrations affected voters during polling, with some confusion about where to vote. Some voters were not allowed to vote as a result of the overall inaccuracy of the voters' roll. The IEC's 2009 performance audit report recommended that the voter registration system be linked to the national identification system, as that would allow voters to use their national identity cards instead of having to carry a separate voter's card (IEC 2010b:41).

Another flaw noted by media was the failure to provide for 3 000 Botswana citizens working in South African mines. They were unable to register to vote in the general elections, despite the fact that the IEC had made provision for other citizens resident in South Africa, including students at tertiary institutions, to register at polling stations near their places of work or study. It would be sensible to debate whether voting stations for citizens living outside Botswana are still needed as the 2009 election report shows that most did not vote: out of 1 644 external voters, only 571 cast their vote (IEC 2010b:73).

Citizens generally are also of the view that, for the IEC to be deemed truly independent, much would have to be changed in the appointment of the Chairperson and Secretary of the IEC, the recruitment of its staff and its accountability system (IEC 2010b:36).

VOTER INFORMATION

27. How much information is conveyed to voters by the official election information system? (6)

In its effort to reach out to all groups of the electorate, the IEC employs every medium available. Posters, booklets and billboards have been used to encourage the electorate to register and vote in the general elections (IEC 2010b:2).

Other strategies employed by the IEC to disseminate election information include *kgotla* meetings, workshops and seminars. The IEC also sponsors a television series called *Matlho-a–Phage*, which brings various stakeholders together to discuss issues of democracy and of national concern. The IEC's use of an outside broadcast vehicle to conduct audio-visual shows in 2009 added a new dimension to its education drive, attracting more people to voter education and information meetings throughout the country (IEC 2010b:38).

To enhance the information dissemination process and make all electoral documents easily accessible, the IEC should publish a compilation of the electoral laws and other texts relating to elections and democracy, which would include the Botswana Constitution, the Electoral Act and codes of electoral conduct. Such a compilation could be very user-friendly to the various stakeholders in elections. Angola produced its own electoral legislation compilation in 2008.

28. How much information about political parties and candidates is conveyed by the news media? And how fairly is this done? (5)

Botswana has a broad and well-defined media regulatory framework in the Code of Conduct for Broadcasters. This code is derived from the mandate of the National Broadcasting Board as set out in the Broadcasting Act (1998). The code encourages equitable and professional treatment of political parties by the media during elections. Among its special provisions for public service broadcasters, it urges them to afford equitable access to all registered political parties and independent candidates. The code provides for an election blackout period of 12 hours, meaning that no party political advertising may be broadcast from 12 hours before the commencement of polling.

There has been general adherence to these provisions, despite the fact that they are guidelines with no legal force. However, incidents of biased reporting in favour of the BDP and of inequitable access by ruling party candidates, especially to the public media, surfaced during the 2009 elections. The opposition Botswana National Front (BNF) filed a complaint with the SADC about what they believed to be unfair treatment by the public broadcaster in covering the party's campaign (Malumo 2009).

29. How much access do political parties have to the media and how equitable is this? (5)

In Botswana, the media are controlled by the State and the private sector. The State uses various media to convey information about political parties, including radio, television and print, all of which have a national reach and are therefore able to communicate to nearly every corner of the country. The State media have always been perceived to be agencies of the ruling party, the BDP, because most of their reports focus on the programmes of government ministers. It is also argued by those with a stake in politics that wide coverage of ministers' schedules by State media is unfair, because the ministers are political appointees who also compete as candidates in elections.

The private media, mainly newspapers and radio stations, afford political parties the opportunity, through their columns and broadcasts, to defend their political policies. The private media's own published opinions and analysis also encourage parties to debate national issues, such as those around the national Constitution. Some newspapers, such as the *Weekend Post* in its 'Presidential Podium' column, have made a deliberate effort to give leaders of all political parties a forum to debate their political programmes. In the 2009 elections, the *Botswana Guardian* introduced constituency political forums in which aspiring candidates across party lines were allowed to defend their political manifestos. Private media editors report, however, that political parties fail to utilise the slots reserved for political opinions adequately. This could be attributable to incompetence on the part of political leaders or to the parties' lack of concrete alternative policies and programmes.

30. To what extent do the campaigns of political parties reach all sections of society? (4)

Botswana's political parties still find it hard to be visible in all regions of the country. In some areas where they claim to have party structures, these have been found to exist in name only. Even though the main political parties (BDP, BNF and Botswana Congress Party (BCP)) have produced manifestos, this hardly guarantees circulation of copies throughout the country (Democracy Research Project 2002:79). The dominant campaigning strategy used by parties is public rallies, followed by house-to-house canvassing and posters of election candidates. Radio, television and newspaper advertisements are expensive and therefore not often used, especially by the opposition.

Table 2.2 shows the impact of financial muscle on successful bids by political parties competing for parliamentary seats in the 2009 national elections.

Table 2.2: Seats contested by parties in 2009 parliamentary elections			
Party	Contested	Won	Percentage
BAM	4	1	1.75
BCP	42	4	7.02
BDP	57	45	78.95
BNF	48	6	10.53
BPP	6	0	0.00
Independent	15	1	1.75
MELS	4	0	0.00
Total	177	57	100
Source: IEC, 2010b.			

31. Do voters know enough about all political parties to be able to make an informed choice? (4)

Elections ought to be about key issues affecting the majority of citizens, such as unemployment, increasing levels of poverty and corruption. However, instead of presenting their visions of the solutions to their country's problems, candidates focus on exploiting the ignorance of the electorate. Instead of attacking policies, they attack their opponents. Instead of clearly outlining how they plan to address the electorate's basic needs, like health, education, jobs, roads, food and a roof over their heads, Botswana politicians are fond of launching sleazy and sensational attacks on opponents in order to make headlines. This situation might explain why the majority of the Botswana electorate find political rallies interesting enough to be worth attending.

The conduct of voters themselves does not help the situation. It is worrying to see them praising and electing candidates only because they come from the same regions.

The media must share the blame because of the way certain politicians are covered. At times, instead of reporting events, the Botswana media add comments about the personalities concerned. For them it is not a question of whose policies might benefit the people, but rather one of who might be taking part in some underhand activity.

The only way to prevent the politics of personal attack becoming an integral part of Botswana's electoral process is for the various stakeholders to take responsibility for ensuring that the public are informed on issue-based politics rather than sleazy and sensational attacks. It starts with the political parties, whose campaigns should only be on concrete policies and issues that directly affect the people and make a direct contribution to their standard of living. Civil society must produce, through voter education, a well-informed population that can discern the relevant issues from the trash. The media have the duty of bringing to citizens a real understanding of each party and individuals standing for public office: what they stand for and their strategies for tackling key issues.

The people must first become better informed about their rights and about the role of a good government, so that they really know what is important when electing anyone to political office. Until the average voter becomes well informed about the role of politics, politicians will continue to engage in personal politics, to everyone's detriment.

ELECTORAL PARTICIPATION

32. How extensively do citizens participate in elections?   (8)

33. How are citizens able to influence the electoral process in ways other than the vote?   (7)

Table 2.3: Registered versus actual voters				
	2004	2009	Absolute change	% increase in voters
Total registered voters	552 849	725 817	172 968	23.83
Total actual voters	421 272	555 308	134 036	24.13

The figures shown in Table 2.3 indicate growth in total voter registration and in total voter turnout, and the voting trend in the 2004 and 2009 elections (IEC 2010b:74).

The IEC had set itself a target of registering 650 000 voters, but in the end managed to register 725 817. Nearly 30% were first-time voters (between the ages of 18 and 29), indicating an unprecedented interest in elections among the youth of Botswana (Democracy Research Project 2002:79). However, it is crucial to state that more effort is still needed to sensitise and mobilise youth participation in elections.

Civil society, through its voter education activities, encourages participation in the electoral process beyond voting. By hosting workshops, forums and debates across the country, civil society targets communities to become involved in the core activities through which the democratic process can be strengthened. Organisations such as the Botswana Electoral Support Network (BESnet) deploy election observers to testify whether or not elections are free and fair. Party agents are also involved in the voting process.

34. To what extent is the management and control of the elections delegated to an independent body?   (5)

As this section has noted, the elections held in Botswana since independence have been free, peaceful and multiparty. Electoral disputes have not yet been accompanied by civil disobedience or the destabilisation of the political system.

The IEC was established by S65A of the Constitution. Its functions entail:

- conducting and supervising elections
- conducting referendums
- ensuring that elections are conducted efficiently, properly, freely and fairly, and
- performing other functions as may be prescribed by an Act of Parliament.

Although the IEC is responsible for the conduct of elections, it does not issue a writ of elections; that is done by the president. This is in conflict with best practice, according to which election dates are fixed in the Constitution. Moreover, the IEC Secretary is appointed by the president, who in essence is a political leader of the ruling party. The IEC's reliance on civil servants, especially district commissioners, council secretaries and other local staff to run elections has led some to suspect the IEC's independence and impartiality (Sebudubudu 2008:120).

In the light of this background information, one can hardly be surprised by the strong perception that the IEC is still not truly independent from the executive. It is important to note, however, that a draft Bill on the independence of the IEC is under consideration; it deals with a number of issues, including the status and membership of the commission, and its functions and powers (IEC 2010b:26).

35. Are there mechanisms for the review of the electoral system and are these open to citizen participation?   (7)

The electoral system can be reviewed during the All-Party Conference and through the Law Reform Committee. The challenges regarding these two structures are, first, that the All-Party Conference appears to be restricted to the appointment of commissioners, and, second, that the Law Reform Committee is charged with too broad a mandate, that of overseeing all legal reforms in the country (IEC 2010b:24).

The IEC's 2009 Performance Audit Team therefore felt that the reform of Botswana's electoral architecture warranted specialised attention through a body such as an electoral reform steering committee (IEC 2010b:24). The team felt that such a body would complement the work of the All-Party Conference and the IEC by acting in an advisory capacity.

That said, the Botswana electoral system has undergone several reforms. These include the setting up of the IEC and its mandate to run the elections, the reduction of the voting age from 21 to 18, voting by proxy and the adoption of ballot papers. In 2008, the Botswana Electoral Act was amended to introduce the separation of certain parliamentary and local elections, in that the Act now stipulates that the counting of votes for parliament and local government shall be done at constituency and polling district headquarters respectively. The effect of these changes was to make the electoral institution independent of government influence, to encourage the youth to exercise their democratic right as soon as they reached maturity, and to expedite the vote-counting process. These reforms involved the public through referendums.

Electoral Outcomes

36. Are the announced election results congruent with how the electorate actually cast their ballots?   (3)

37. Do citizens believe that their vote makes a difference?   (5)

38. Do security forces, the government and political parties accept the election results?   (8)

39. Do citizens accept the election results?   (8)

Botswana's use of the FPTP electoral mechanism makes the losers feel disempowered and alienated from the political system. It inspires confidence and trust in the supporters of the dominant party and a sense of exclusion in the supporters of the losing parties (Molomo 2005:37).

Historically, Botswana's general elections have not been without contestation. Some election petitions have been through the courts seeking the rejection of electoral outcomes. These include the most famous successful parliamentary petition for Gaborone South in 1984 and that for Mochudi in 1989. Election petitions demonstrate the dissatisfaction that remains after elections. It is worth noting that, while the laws of Botswana provide for election results to be challenged in court, the court process is not only expensive, but also time-consuming. What is needed, therefore, is a way of solving electoral disputes quickly. It has been observed over the years that most petitions to come before the courts have failed on technical grounds (IEC 2010b:57). The 2009 audit team recommended the legal enforcement of the code of conduct, the establishment of a unit within the IEC with powers to deal with electoral complaints, and the strengthening of the party liaison committees as a first port of call before petitioners seek recourse to the High Court.

Botswana's positive record of being able to conduct free and peaceful elections with decreasing contestation over election results indicates widespread public acceptance of the electoral process and results. Botswana's electoral history shows a steady growth in voter registration and turnout since the 1979 elections, and does not reflect voter alienation.

There is also no record of complaints that the security agencies have ever disrupted the electoral process.

Table 2.4: Registration and voting trends			
Year	Registered	Voted	%
1965	188 950	140 858	74.55
1969	140 428	76 858	54.73
1974	205 050	64 011	31.22
1979	230 231	134 496	58.42
1984	293 571	227 756	77.58
1989	367 069	250 487	68.24
1994	370 173	283 375	76.55
1999	459 662	354 466	77.11
2004	552 849	421 272	76.20
2009	725 817	555 308	76.51
Source: IEC 2010b.			

40. How closely do the composition of the legislatures and the selection of government reflect the election outcome? (3)

41. How far do the legislatures reflect the social composition of the electorate? To what extent are women represented in parliament? (3)

The FPTP electoral system that Botswana uses makes it impossible for the composition of the legislatures to reflect the election outcome. As discussed earlier, the FPTP system does not provide for effective political representation; local council and parliamentary electoral outcomes do not reflect the broad interests represented in society.

Despite the pluralism manifested by the existence of several political parties, Botswana's electoral system has ensured that, in terms of parliamentary seats, the ruling party, the BDP, has won all elections by decisive majorities. As recorded in Table 2.1, in the 2009 elections the BDP won 45 seats, the BNF six, the BCP four, and the Botswana Alliance Movement (BAM) and an independent candidate one each. If, on the other hand, a proportional representation system had been used, the BDP would have won 30 seats and the combined opposition, 27. It is strongly contended that the FPTP electoral system creates a feeling of exclusion among those who vote for opposition parties.

The president is indirectly elected by virtue of being the presidential candidate of the parliamentary majority. Although the president is not directly elected, he wields extensive executive powers which come directly from the Constitution and not from parliament.

The current electoral system cannot ensure gender equality in parliament. In a parliament of 61 members, there are only four women, two of whom are specially elected (i.e., appointed by the president). The insignificant level of representation of women in parliament is largely explained by the infrequent nomination of women candidates by political parties.

Table 2.5 sets out the history of women's representation in Botswana parliamentary politics.

Table 2.5: Representation of women in parliament			
Year	Total seats	Women's seats	% women
2009	61	4	6.56
2004	61	7	11.48
1999	44	8	18.18
1994	44	4	9.09
1989	38	2	5.26
1984	38	ND	ND
1979	36	ND	ND
1974	36	ND	ND
1969	35	0	0
1965	35	ND	ND
Note: ND = No data.			
Source: Electoral Institute of Southern Africa.			

Overall, it is argued that Botswana opposition parties suffer many disabilities emanating from the FPTP electoral system, including the effects of legislative bodies being formed that do not reflect the popular vote and the will of the people. The opposition parties and civil society organisations have, over the years, argued for the reform of the system, proposing either proportional representation or a mixed-member proportional system.

FUNDING ELECTIONS

42. To what extent are private donations to political parties permitted and are they subject to regulation (such as transparency and limits), in order to prevent them from having a disproportionate impact on voter choice and electoral outcome?   (3)

43. Is campaign finance – both income and expenditure – regulated?   (4) Are the political parties regulated by accepted procedures and non-partisan bodies? How extensive is the independent oversight of election expenditure?   (5)

44. Is there public financing of political parties?   (0)

Botswana has no legislation regulating the private funding of political parties. The electoral law does not stop political parties from securing external funding, nor does it regulate external funding. The current Electoral Act only specifies the level of election expenses per candidate, but even this is not strictly adhered to (Molomo & Sebudubudu 2005:150). In terms of the Electoral Act, each candidate is only allowed a maximum of 50 000 Pula as election expenses (ROB 1968:S81). But there are cases of the BDP having received huge amounts of money in donations from local and international sources and donors. The absence of a law requiring political parties to declare their sources of funding effectively undermines issues of national security and interest. There is therefore an increasingly urgent need to introduce a law that forces parties to disclose their sources of funding.

The Botswana Electoral Act provides for the disclosure of expenditure and returns of election expenses. S84(1) reads:

All money provided by an association or group of persons or by any person for the election expenses of a candidate, whether a gift, loan, advance or deposit, … shall be fully disclosed.

Furthermore, S87(1) requires every election candidate to submit to the returning officer, within 90 days of the result of the election being declared, a true return of all expenses pertaining to the election.

It has been observed, however, that the law on election expenses is inadequate as it does not address the disclosure of sources of election funding and how such money may be spent during election campaigns. Regarding the independent oversight of election expenditure, the Electoral Act empowers the Secretary of the IEC to enforce the election expenses clause (ROB 1968:S87(1)). However, although politicians are required by law to declare their election expenses, they do not always do so. Some stakeholders say this could be due to the fact that they are not reimbursed and therefore do not see it as important to account for their expenses. From this situation arises the need to put in place a strict code of financial regulation to ensure a level political playing field.

If Botswana introduced the public financing of political parties, that would allow the parties to compete effectively and fairly, because they would all be able to finance their campaigns, print campaign material, use billboards, distribute flyers and advertise in the media. Through such funding, political parties would be able to maintain a certain level of political visibility, especially in rural areas, where many roads can only be traversed by high-performance vehicles. It would also enhance the ability of the electorate to make more informed choices by giving them better access to information.

It can therefore be concluded that the principle of public funding for political parties in Botswana has to be applied, because promoting the key tenets of liberal democracies, transparency and accountability requires better-resourced parties.

Conclusion

Despite the challenges in the wider political landscape of the country, elections in Botswana have, judging from the reports of analysts and observers, been peaceful and well managed. The IEC appears to enjoy widespread support from all electoral stakeholders and is considered credible and efficient in the exercise of its mandate and functions. Electoral disputes have not yet entailed civil disobedience or destabilisation of the political system.

However, there are gaps in Botswana's electoral system which need to be addressed in order to strengthen the country's democratic elections. Desirable electoral reforms would include:

- reforming the current FPTP electoral system to include more women, more young people and minority groups such as people with disability in decision-making structures

- amending the Constitution to provide for the election of the president by popular vote and to stipulate a fixed date for national elections

- amending the Electoral Act to enhance the status of the IEC as an independent, robust authority able to deliver credible elections

- introducing State funding for political parties so as to consolidate competitive politics

- amending the electoral law to provide for reporting on private party funding and spending, and

- incorporating the codes of conduct for political parties and the media into the legal framework to give these instruments legal force.

In addition there is the need for increased voter education by the IEC for voters with special needs, such as the visually impaired. To ensure that the voting process is inclusive and effective, mobile voting stations have to be introduced (requiring amendment of the Electoral Act) to cater for eligible bedridden patients in hospitals and home-based care programmes. The mobile voting stations should also be available to voters who cannot reach their voting stations. The Electoral Act needs to be amended to guarantee the right of employees in the private sector to time off for voting on election day. In order to reduce the time taken to process election petitions to less than 90 days, as is currently the case, Botswana should consider designing and introducing an improved complaints system and incorporating it into the election legislation.

Endnote

1. We would like to thank the following for validating information in this section: Mr Moeti Mohwasa, publicity secretary, BNF; Political Education Office, BDP; Mr Thato Osupile, administrative secretary, BCP; Mr Osupile Maroba, IEC principal public relations officer; Ms Hilda B Modisane, programme officer, Electoral Commissions Forum of SADC Countries; Mr Tomeletso Sereri, editor, *The Echo*; Mr Ntibinyane Ntibinyane, reporter, *Botswana Guardian*; Mr Kealeboga Morapedi, youth activist.

SECTION THREE

ACCOUNTABILITY AND DEMOCRACY

BY EMMANUEL BOTLHALE

Accountability is one of the key tenets of democracy and operates on two levels: the political and the administrative. Accountability comports with democracy in the sense that the governed need to know what is done in their name. In addition, it is a key requirement of good governance (Corkery 1999; Kaul 2000; UNESCAP 2010). Hence, accountability should enhance democracy and good governance.

Unlike the city states of ancient Greece, in which citizens exercised direct democracy, modern society has imperatives that necessitate indirect democracy. Thus, citizens surrender their sovereign rights to make decisions to certain members of society chosen through an election. The representatives are in most instances councillors of local authorities and Members of Parliament (MPs). Since political representatives make decisions, such as allocating resources to programmes and projects, on behalf of citizens, citizens legitimately expect accountability measures to be in place so that representatives can account for those decisions. But modern governments need an army of bureaucrats to implement public policies and programmes: to spend the budget, enforce the rule of law, collect taxes and so on. In carrying out these functions the bureaucrats are, in effect, agents acting on behalf of their principals, the citizens – and principals legitimately expect an agent to account for actions taken on their behalf.

This section examines the adequacy of various institutions in ensuring democratic accountability in Botswana. It considers, among other things, the role of parliament as an oversight body, political and administrative accountability, popular participation, the budgetary process and access to information. It concludes by discussing key issues that constrain accountability, democracy and good governance.

Executive accountability and legislative oversight

45. How far is the executive subject to the rule of law and transparent rules of government in the use of its powers? To what extent are all public officials subject to the rule of law and to transparent rules in the performance of their functions?   (7)

Typical of democracies, there is a separation of powers in Botswana between the three arms of government – the legislature, the executive and the judiciary. The bodies are functionally independent, so none should interfere with the functions and powers of the others. The legislature makes laws, the judiciary interprets and implements laws, and the executive, being the operational arm of the government, must act according to the law and, on the whole, does so. In a dispensation characterised by the rule of law, administrative action falls within the ambit of the law. In this regard, the 2011 public sector strike offers an instructive lesson on the operation of the rule of law on the part of the executive. Since the passage of the Public Service Act (2008) (ROB 2008b), which created a unified public service, all public servants have had the right to engage in legal strike action. Following stalled salary negotiations between the Botswana Federation of Public Employees Organisations (BOFEPUSO) and the Directorate of Public Service Management (DPSM) in February 2011, the federation embarked on a legal – and therefore protected – strike from 18 April to 13 June.[1] The DPSM and BOFEPUSO agreed on strike rules and procedures, including the proviso that essential workers such as those in the electricity, fire, health, sewerage, water, transport and telecommunications services should not participate in the strike.[2]

When the strike got under way, some essential services workers joined it. Instead of summarily firing them, the government went to court to force them out of the strike. On 26 April 2011, the Industrial Court ruled that the strike action by essential workers was both unlawful and unprotected.[3] It argued that the said workers could not join the strike because that was in contravention of the Trade Disputes Act (2004), and ordered them to go back to work.[4] On 6 May 2011, the same court confirmed the 26 April interim order.[5] Unfortunately, some essential services employees did not obey the court order and, consequently, were fired from their jobs (Galeitse 2011a). At the time of writing, the dismissed workers had yet to appeal against their dismissal (Galeitse 2011b), but the government was expected to comply with the result of any appeal.

All public officials are subject to the rule of law, in the sense that the Public Service Act governs them. The amended Public Service Act (No. 30 of 2008), commenced on 1 May 2010 and provides for a single law governing the employment of all government employees.[6] Certain organisations are governed by specific Acts, such as the Botswana Defence Force (BDF), which is governed by the Botswana Defence Force Act (1977). Thus, public officers who contravene the law invariably face legal consequences. To illustrate: on 25 November 2005, members of the Botswana Police Service and BDF allegedly forced some Zimbabwean nationals to perform sex acts. The matter reached the courts because the victims claimed that the officers had been acting outside the ambit of the law (Mooketsi 2007). Another familiar and recent case is that of John Kalafatis, for whose murder four BDF personnel were convicted on 13 May 2009 (Morewagae 2011b).

The law provides for public officials to act in accordance with the rule of law, but there is only an implied requirement and expectation that they act transparently, as Botswana has no freedom of information Act. Although innumerable representations have been made over the years for the introduction of such legislation, the government has not acceded to these demands. However, it finally conceded to discussion of an Act in early 2011.

After the Attorney-General's office drafted a proposed freedom of information Act, the Media Institute of Southern Africa (Botswana Chapter) organised a stakeholders' meeting on 21 April 2011 to discuss the draft (Motseta 2011). Among the meeting's key observations were that the draft legislation did not apply to private entities (e.g. political parties) and that the Office of the President was shielded from the proposed Act in respect of presidential commissions. On 8 July 2011, in terms of Standing Order 60(2), parliament allowed the Botswana Congress Party's Dumelang Saleshando to present the Freedom of Information Bill as a private member's Bill during the November sitting of parliament (ROB 2011). Notably, the Bill intends 'to extend the right of members of the public to access information in the possession of public authorities' (ROB 2011: b.315). Hence, in the absence of a freedom of information Act, and noting that instruments such as the Media Practitioners Act (2009), Intelligence and Security Act (2007) and National Security Act (1986) place constraints on the free flow of information, there are transparency challenges. The adoption of this Freedom of Information Bill is therefore imperative because it will bring some accountability and transparency in the conduct of public affairs (Botlhale 2011a).

46. How extensive and effective are the legislature's powers to scrutinise the executive, hold it to account, and initiate and scrutinise, as well as amend, legislation between elections? Is the legislature able to hold the executive to account for the implementation of legislation and policy? (5)

Botswana operates a Westminster system, which, by its nature, creates a very strong executive, particularly in the Cabinet. The Cabinet, appointed by the president, is drawn from parliament, and at the time of writing there were 21 ministers and assistant ministers. This heavy front-bench complement makes it very difficult for the legislature to provide an effective check on the Cabinet. As for accountability, ministers respond to questions asked by Members of Parliament (MPs), for which purpose parliament recently amended its standing orders to set aside Fridays as question time. These question-and-answer sessions allow the MPs to ask ministers questions, but the process could be improved in line with Prime Minister's Question Time in the United Kingdom's House of Commons: every Wednesday, when the House of Commons is sitting, the Prime Minister spends half an hour answering questions from MPs. In Botswana's case, the president should similarly attend parliament on an appointed day and respond to questions from MPs.

Although parliament is vested with powers to call anyone, including the president, to account for omissions and commissions within the scope of their official duties, it rarely, if ever, does that. Thus parliament robs itself of the chance to call the executive to account for the implementation of legislation and policy – before, during and after implementation. As it is, the executive, and in particular the Cabinet, accounts to the president and reports neither to parliament nor to special parliamentary committees afterwards. The only time that the Cabinet accounts to parliament in regard to the implementation of legislation and policy is when MPs ask questions. Hence, the reporting is done on a 'need to know' basis.

47. To what extent has legislative and executive power been devolved and what impact has this had on popular control? (4)

Although Botswana is a unitary State, the intention to devolve powers to sub-national governments came about as a result of the Local Government (District Councils) and Townships Act (1965). The Act created rural and urban councils, which function as mediums of decentralisation (Mfundisi 1998). Similar intentions came by way of the Decentralisation in Botswana: Policy Paper and Action Plan (1993). Furthermore, there were presidential commissions on local government structure in Botswana in 1979 and 2001 (MLGL 1979; MLGL 2001) that looked into devolving powers to the councils. The official policy is that the government is committed to the devolution of legislative and executive power to sub-national governments.[7] However, the truth is that this is largely symbolic, because the sub-national governments depend on subventions from the central government, and this financial dependence puts paid to efforts to devolve legislative and executive powers to them (Loaneka 2003). If anything, there has been deconcentration, 'the weakest form of decentralisation that involves a shift of the workload from the central authorities or from the central headquarters to the local officials' (Uwadibie 1999:55), and sub-national governments are consequently extensions of the central government (Picard 1979).

PUBLIC PARTICIPATION AND ACCOUNTABILITY

48. How open, accessible, extensive and systematic are the procedures/ mechanisms for public consultation and participation in legislation and policy-making? How equal is the access which interest groups/citizens have to influence the law-making process? (6)

Building on the tradition of *therisanyo* (consultation and consensus-building), consultation and participation should guide legislation and policy making. It is one of the original four national principles of Botswana, the others being democracy, development and self-reliance. In this regard, the *kgotla* (public meeting place) serves as the village parliament. This is where all village people gather, presided over by a tribal head (headman or chief), to discuss communal issues. The tribal head listens to all contributions and, afterwards, summarises them and formulates a majority or consensus position.

Still building on the *therisanyo* principle, the government introduced *dipitso* (public opinion-gathering forums) in 2010 as exemplified by the sports *pitso*, water *pitso* and energy *pitso*. These are occasions on which stakeholders meet to provide input into policy making. For example, in 2010, after 44 years of independence, the Ministry of Finance and Development Planning (MFDP) opened up the budget formulation process to the public through budget *dipitso*, which thus informed the 2011–12 budget speech and budget (Matambo 2011).

However, this is not to say that the *dipitso* have replaced long-standing consultative forums such as workshops. For instance, the Public Enterprises Evaluation and Privatisation Agency held a stakeholders' consultative workshop on 19 September 2011 to discuss the draft Privatisation Master Plan II 2012–2017. Other consultative forums are the High Level Consultative Council (HLCC), the National AIDS Council and district development planning conferences. The HLCC, which meets twice a year and is chaired by the president of Botswana, is attended by all ministries and their top policy-making officials, as well as captains of industry who represent the private sector. The HLCC sits to consider many national issues.

There are challenges, though. For instance, some Batswana feel that there are government officials who talk at, rather than with, the people during *kgotla* meetings. For all its imperfections, such as low attendance by the youth and the exclusion of ethnic 'minorities'[8] (Mompati & Prinsen 2000), and despite some doubts as to whether it is an effective consultative forum (Lekorwe 1989), the *pitso* is an enduring consultative forum (Khama 2010). President Ian Khama emphasised its centrality when delivering the 2011 State of the Nation address. He said, 'I along with my fellow Cabinet members have found it odd that some have even criticised us for taking certain issues to *dikgotla* around the country, which since time immemorial have remained the bedrock for community discourse on all matters of public concern' (Khama 2011:para. 9).

49. How open, accessible, extensive and systematic are the procedures/ mechanisms for public consultation and participation in executive policy? And how equal is the access which citizens have to influence executive policy?   (6)

The separation of powers doctrine means that the legislature formulates laws and policies, while the executive implements them. At times, however, ministers – that is, the executive – propose laws and policies that they bring to parliament for adoption. It is a legal requirement in Botswana that, before bringing a Bill to parliament, the responsible minister must consult with relevant stakeholders, so as to allow them input into the Bill. For example, following the 2011 public sector unions' strike, the government moved swiftly to expand the list of essential services workers. On 6 July 2011, however, parliament rejected Statutory Instrument Number 49, through which the then Minister of Labour and Home Affairs, Peter Siele, sought to amend the Trade Disputes Act (2004) to make teachers, diamond sorters and veterinarians essential service workers.[9] Opponents of the move argued that Siele had not consulted all the relevant stakeholders, particularly trade unions and the Labour Advisory Board. The 'government'[10] was not happy with the decision,[11] so Siele went back to parliament on 3 August 2011 and re-tabled the amendment to the Trade Disputes Act (2004).[12] Yet again, some MPs, particularly those from opposition parties, complained that Siele had not consulted with relevant stakeholders. Siele admitted that he had not had time to consult sufficiently, but, despite these misgivings, the Bill was voted into law.[13]

The budget *dipitso* are further examples of processes that enable both male and female members of the public to participate in public policy. Prior to late 2010, budget preparation was virtually the preserve of the bureaucracy, in particular the MFDP (Botlhale 2010b). Following calls for the opening up of the budgetary process, the MFDP introduced budget *dipitso* in 2010, and two were held: one on 28 October, which the author attended, and the other in November, specifically for MPs. At the October event, Finance Ministry officials explained the purpose of the *pitso*: to democratise the budgetary process in Botswana, mainly through popular participation and transparency. Then Assistant Finance Minister, Charles Tibone, said, 'As a country, we want a credible and transparent budgeting system that accommodates the views of Batswana' (Tibone 2010:2).

These cases demonstrate that there are mechanisms for public consultation and participation on executive policy in Botswana – and yet there are some instances of citizens feeling that certain ministers either do not consult relevant stakeholders or do so only superficially. A case in point was that of the proposed regulations in terms of the Liquor Trade Act (2007). It was widely held that the then Assistant Minister of Trade and Industry, Duke Lefhoko, had not adequately consulted relevant stakeholders when he sought to introduce these regulations, which included shorter liquor trading hours. It was further contended that Lefhoko was acting at the behest of President Ian Khama, an anti-alcohol crusader (Khama 2008b). Hard on the heels of the amended regulations to the Liquor Trade Act (2007), the government introduced a 30% alcohol levy on 1 November 2008.[14] Similar charges were levelled at Lefhoko on that occasion.

50. How far does government cooperate with relevant partners, associations and communities in forming and carrying out policies and how far are people able to participate in these processes? (6)

There are essentially two sets of players in the field of public administration: State and non-State actors. As stated elsewhere, *therisanyo* is the key guiding principle in the conduct of public affairs. Through *therisanyo*, public space is opened up for the non-State actors. In this regard, an array of consultative forums is employed to operationalise *therisanyo*, including *kgotla* meetings, stakeholder workshops, district conferences, the HLCC, the National AIDS Council and *dipitso*. In addition, members of the community are free to make representations to their representatives (local authority councillors and MPs).

Not that these arrangements are perfect; there are challenges around them. In particular, some sceptics dismiss such attempts as whitewashing exercises (Noppen 1982). At the same time, as demonstrated by the recent public-sector strike, the frontiers of consultation need to be extended. In this regard, forums such as the all-party conferences must be resuscitated. (Inexplicably, these have been stopped.[15])

LAW-MAKING AND THE BUDGET PROCESS

51. How extensive are the powers of legislative bodies, and how effective are they at legislating? (5)

Even though the Constitution of Botswana vests all law-making powers in the legislature, there is an overlap between the legislature and executive in the sense that all 21 ministers and assistant ministers are drawn from the 57 elected MPs. Thanks to these numbers, the front bench often tilts the vote in favour of the government. In addition, the ruling Botswana Democratic Party (BDP) operates a caucus system that makes its decisions binding on MPs. Those who defy caucus decisions do so at considerable risk, as the case of Pono Moatlhodi demonstrates (Nkala 2008). In November 2008, Moatlhodi was reprimanded for undermining a caucus decision by speaking over the time limit and maligning the BDP. Consequently he was recalled as a parliamentary candidate and was only allowed to stand again as a MP after apologising to the party leadership. Similarly, when the BDP held its national congress on 29 July 2011, it instructed the MPs to support Siele's amendments to the Trade Disputes Act (2004). Indeed, a majority of the BDP MPs voted on the government side.

These case studies demonstrate the fact that, although the legislature is vested with law-making powers, such powers can be circumscribed by one-party dominance and an overbearing party leadership.

52. How rigorous are the procedures for parliamentary approval, supervision of and input into the budget and public expenditure? (6)

The budget process is governed by two pieces of legislation: S119 of the Constitution (ROB 1997) and the Finance and Audit Act (2003) (ROB 2003). For example, the Constitution enjoins the Minister of Finance and Development Planning to submit estimates of government revenue and expenditure to the National Assembly before the start of each financial year. The estimates are tabled in the National Assembly 14 days in advance, and the Finance Minister presents the Appropriation Bill for the first reading and delivers the budget speech. On completion of the budget speech, the revenue estimates are tabled and the Appropriation Bill is read for the second time. After debates, the Bill is read for the third time and, when it is approved, it is referred to the president for signing. Once signed, the Bill becomes an Appropriation Act.

Despite this elaborate institutional arrangement, parliament's budget amendment powers are limited (CABRI 2008). The legislature can amend the proposed budget but cannot change the deficit or surplus amount and, if the proposed budget is not approved by the legislature on 1 April, the Finance Minister's proposal stands. Given party caucus systems in which caucus decisions 'de-tongue' MPs by instructing them how to debate the budget speech (in essence, to approve it uncritically), the power of the purse is largely symbolic (Botlhale 2010b).

53. **How much say does the public have in the development of the budget? How well do parliamentary procedures allow the public to participate in decisions relating to resource allocation?** (7)

Prior to the introduction of budget *dipitso* in 2010, the preparation of the budget was virtually the preserve of the MFDP and a few other players, so budget participation was minimal[16] (Phirinyane 2005). Notably, the *dipitso* enable all stakeholders to take part in the budgetary process. It is too early to judge the efficacy of the *dipitso* as they are fairly new, but they are a step in the right direction.

Access to Information

54. **How independent and accessible is public information about government policies and actions and their effects? How comprehensive and effective is legislation giving citizens the right of access to government information?** (4)

In the absence of freedom of information legislation, and given the existence of instruments such as the Media Practitioners Act (2009), the Intelligence and Security Act (2007) and the National Security Act (1986) that place constraints on the free flow of information, there are transparency challenges. The passage of the Freedom of Information Bill and the review, if not repeal, of these Acts is therefore imperative.

Accessibility and Independence

55. **How accessible are elected representatives to members of the public? What impact does the electoral and party system have on the way in which MPs represent people?** (8)

Under the single-member constituency/ward system, elected representatives are geographically tied to their constituencies and wards. MPs and councillors therefore have a direct link with the electorate, which makes them easily accessible. It is not uncommon for the electorate to have the cellphone numbers of their representatives. Added to that, the councillors are closest to the electorate because they reside either in or near the same places as the electorate.

56. How far are MPs protected from undue influence by outside interests? Are potential conflicts of interest regulated? (8)

Although campaign finance is loosely regulated in Botswana – for instance, there is no requirement to disclose sources of funds – there are no documented cases of undue influence by outside interests. As for conflicts of interest, MPs are required by regulation to declare their interests: for example, they may not sit and deliberate in a meeting if they have some interest in the matter at hand, and must recuse themselves.

57. How effective is the separation of public office, elected and unelected, from party advantage and the personal, business and family interests of office holders? (7)

Public and private lives are kept separate through an assortment of laws (for example, the general orders governing appointments to public office). Over and above this, oversight bodies such as the Office of the Ombudsman and the Directorate on Corruption and Economic Crime curb corrupt practices. For example, a minister and a former minister stood trial on corruption charges in 2011.[17]

58. How independent are the judiciary and the courts from the executive and from all kinds of interference? (8)

The judiciary is independent and the government does not interfere with its work.[18] Furthermore, judges enjoy security of tenure. Importantly, the judges are appointed by the president upon recommendation by the Judicial Service Commission (JSC). Recently, however, there have been charges that President Khama, contrary to long-standing tradition, sometimes does not endorse the recommendations of the JSC. His refusal to confirm Gabriel Rwelengera as a judge or to appoint Gabriel Komboni and Lizo Ngcongco as acting judges are cases in point (Modise & Mosikare 2009). In addition, past practice was that, for a given number of vacancies, the JSC would recommend exactly that number of candidates. Lately, however, the president has required the JSC to put forward a greater number of candidates so that he can pick and choose from among them.

59. How effective and open to scrutiny is the control exercised by the legislature and the executive over civil servants? (7)

Civil servants do not report to parliament. However, accounting officers (i.e. permanent secretaries) do report to it through the Public Accounts Committee. Regarding the executive, there is a hierarchal structure, with the permanent secretary to the president at the top of the pyramid. Then there is the Directorate of Public Service Management (DPSM), which is responsible for the appointment, promotion, transfer, dismissal and discipline of public servants.[19]

60. How far is the influence of powerful corporations and business interests over public policy kept in check, and how free are they from involvement in corruption?   (8)

No documentation exists relating to the nexus between business and democracy. De Beers, a powerful corporation, has not been accused of influence-peddling, save that it allegedly sponsored the BDP and its then leader, Ketumile Masire, in the 1990s (Kelebonye 2010).

61. To what extent is the public service protected from corrupt practices? To what extent are public officials protected from undue influence by outside interests? Are potential conflicts of interest regulated?   (7)

Corruption is kept in check by an assortment of laws and regulations, including government general orders, as well as courts and oversight bodies such as the Directorate on Corruption and Economic Crime. These tools also protect public officials from undue influence by outside interests. Potential conflicts of interest are regulated by regulations on the disclosure of interests.

According to recent editions of the Transparency International Corruption Perceptions Index, corruption is not a major problem in Botswana.[20] This notwithstanding, there have been instances of senior public officials being prosecuted for corruption. These include Michael Tshipinare, then Minister of Local Government, Lands and Housing (*Tshipinare v The State*),[21] and Victor Rantshabeng, Deputy Permanent Secretary in the Ministry of Labour and Home Affairs.[22] In addition, there are allegations of corruption at the Botswana Development Corporation (Balise 2011) and the Botswana Export Development and Investment Authority.[23]

62. Are public servants who blow the whistle on corruption encouraged and protected? Are citizens who blow the whistle on corruption protected?   (7)

Public servants and citizens who blow the whistle on corruption are encouraged, but are minimally protected. This is so because there are no whistle-blower protection laws, but merely a promise from law enforcement officers that whistle-blowers' identities will not be revealed. Commendably, though, a whistle-blower protection law is being crafted (Khama 2011).

63. To what extent can the government carry out its responsibilities in accordance with the wishes of the citizens, free of interference or constraint from political or economic forces outside of Botswana?   (8)

Botswana is a sovereign country, therefore it does not take direction from foreign political or economic forces. In this regard, there is nothing documented to suggest that the State has had to do anything to appease foreign political or economic forces. The government has a long-standing relationship with De Beers, but this is a mutually beneficial partnership between consenting parties and, importantly, De Beers does not influence economic policy.

64. **How far is the government able to influence or control those things that are most important to the lives of its people, and how well is it organised, informed and resourced to do so?** (9)

Botswana was poor when it gained independence on 30 September 1966 (Acemoglu *et al.* 2003; Edge 1998; Tsie 1998). Therefore, from day one, the country unremittingly set itself on a path of development, despite unfavourable conditions with zero investable resources (Maipose 2008). When minerals were discovered, particularly diamonds in the 1970s, proceeds from their sale were invested in the economy, and specifically in infrastructure, education and health. Thus, Botswana graduated from the ranks of low-income countries in 1992 to become a middle-income economy (Mogae 2006), and now aspires to be a high-income society (Khama 2011). During the recent global economic downturn, the government chose to run budget deficits from 2008 to 2011 to keep the economy afloat, but it has vowed to restore fiscal balance in 2012 (Botlhale 2011b; MFDP, 2010; MFDP 2011a; MFDP 2011b).

CONCLUSION

This chapter has reviewed Botswana's performance by using various indicators of account-ability and democracy. The review is premised on the conviction that accountability is one of the key tenets of democracy. In fact, accountability is a democratic right. Overall, Botswana scores favourably in the assessment (7/10). However, serious challenges remain: parliament is weak (Molomo 2000), and only nominally independent, so it is subject to the whims and caprices of the executive; attempts at decentralisation are half-hearted; and there is no budget Act to provide for, among other things, a system of public expenditure tracking by non-governmental organisations. To enhance accountability, democracy and good governance, thoroughgoing reforms are needed to address these three concerns – and the strengthening of parliament should top the list.

ENDNOTES

1   http://www.gov.bw/Global/DPSM/press.pdf?epslanguage=en, http://www.yaronafm.co.bw/news/public-sector-unions-continue-with-strike-as-impasse-is-reached-yet-again-1; Baputaki (2011).

2   http://www.gov.bw/en/Ministries--Authorities/Ministries/State-President/Office-of-the-President/Tools--Services/NewsPress-Releases/Government-and-Unions-agree-on-strike-rules/

3   http://www.gov.bw/en/Ministries--Authorities/Ministries/State-President/Office-of-the-President/Tools--Services/NewsPress-Releases/Industrial-Court-Rules-Strike-by-Essential-Workers-Illegal-/

4   http://www.gov.bw/en/News/Go-back-to-work/

5   http://www.gov.bw/en/Ministries--Authorities/Ministries/State-President/Office-of-the-President/Tools--Services/NewsPress-Releases/Industrial-Court-Rules-Strike-by-Essential-Workers-Illegal-/

6   http://www.gov.bw/en/Ministries--Authorities/Ministries/State-President/Office-of-the-President/Tools--Services/NewsPress-Releases/The-Amended-Public-Service-Act-070510/

7   Botswana Press Agency. 2000. 'Decentralisation is Essential' in *Daily News*, 20 December 2000:1.

8   This refers mainly to people such as the Bakgalagadi and Basarwa (San). However, the term is heavily disputed.

9   Anon. 2011. 'Siele Dumps New Act' in *Mmegi*, 7 July 2011:1.

10 It is not clear what the Office of the President meant by 'government' in this news release. It is generally conjectured that it was referring to the Cabinet.

11 http://www.gov.bw/en/Ministries--Authorities/Ministries/State-President/Office-of-the-President/Tools--Services/NewsPress-Releases/Government-disappointed-by-annulment-of-Statutory-Instrument-on-Essential-Services-/

12 Botswana Press Agency. 2011. 'Trade Disputes Act back' in *Daily News*, 5 August 2011:1; Botswana Press Agency. 2011. 'Minister Siele defends decision to amend Act' in *Daily News*, 8 August 2011:4; http://bit.ly/GPUUA7.

13 Piet (2011b); Botswana Press Agency. 2011: 'Parliament expands essential services cadre' in *Daily News*, 18 August 2011:1.

14 Botswana Press Agency. 2008. '30% levy on: come November 1' in *Daily News*, 20 October 2008:1.

15 Botswana Press Agency. 2011. 'No plans to convene all-party conference' in *Daily News*, 11 August 2011:2.

16 Botswana Press Agency. 2007. 'Parliament wants to play an active role' in *Daily News*, 14 February 2007:4; Botswana Press Agency. 2010. 'Public involvement in budget formulation critical' in Daily News, 6 February 2010:2; Radio Botswana. 2010. News at 7 a.m., 17 February 2010; *Sunday Standard*. 2006. 'Parliament's involvement in preparing the national budget is overdue', 14 December 2006:4; *Sunday Standard*. 2009. 'Public hearings can shore up Botswana's budget transparency', 13–19 February 2009:4.

17 *Mmegi*. 2010. 'Seretse stands accused', 2 September 2010:1; *Mmegi*. 2011. 'Minister Matambo charged', 17 May 2011:1.

18 Botswana Press Agency. 2011. 'Judiciary is independent' in *Daily News*, 24 October 2011:2.

19 http://www.dpsm.gov.bw/index.php?option=com_content&view=article&id=83&Itemid=29

20 http://www.gov.bw/en/Business/Topics/Fighting-Corruption-and-Money-Laundering/Low-corruption-level-in-Botswana/

21 BLR 434. Tshipinare was acquitted on appeal.

22 Morewagae, I. 2011b. 'Jamali, Rantshabeng Acquitted' in *Mmegi*, 3 October 2011:1. Rantshabeng was acquitted on a technicality.

23 Botswana Press Agency. 2011: 'BEDIA hands over report' in *Daily News*, 18 August 2011:1.

SECTION FOUR

POLITICAL FREEDOMS AND DEMOCRACY

BY THAPELO NDLOVU

Botswana is one of the most politically stable countries in Africa. On gaining independence in 1966, the country immediately adopted the multiparty system, against the trend of one-party States prevailing across the continent.

Elections held at five-year intervals have entrenched confidence in Botswana's system and attracted accolades on the continent and beyond. The regular changes in the office of Head of State since the tenure of President Sir Ketumile Masire have made the system more trustworthy. The international community has questioned neither the quality of the democracy, nor the country's human rights record, always comparing them favourably with the situation in the rest of Africa. Little attention has been given to the fact that, over the years, Botswana has actually become a *de facto* one-party State. The former United States ambassador, Mr Joseph Huggins, observed that the approach of the ruling Botswana Democratic Party (BDP) to governance was assimilationist and aimed at extending executive power (US

Embassy Gaborone 2005). This shift has been attributed to weak opposition parties that are not able to challenge the ruling party at national level (Phirinyane *et al.* 2006).

It is however submitted that Botswana never had the key characteristics usually identified with proper respect for human rights or democracy. Most conspicuous in its absence is a human rights commission (Ombudsman, annual report 2004). Another democratic defect is that the ruling party has always enjoyed unfair access to State resources, particularly the State media, which is the most powerful weapon for a political player. Further, few African countries have progressed enough to accept the importance of capable opposition parties. Many ruling parties in Africa, including Botswana, take advantage of resource-poor opposition parties that are unable to take them to task effectively. Opposition parties are unable to access State broadcasters, which makes it difficult for them to reach remote populations (Teshome B. 2009).

Over the years, Botswana's democracy has stagnated and, in some respects, actually showed signs of regression. A number of observers point to the Constitution, which is viewed as archaic and not progressive (Botswana Congress Party n.d.). In a recent paper, three University of Botswana academics, Mokganedi Zara Botlhomilwe, Professor David Sebudubudu and Bugalo Maripe, observe that 'Botswana can no longer be regarded as an "African miracle" given that the new democratic regimes in the region have surpassed her in upholding basic democratic principles' (Botlhomilwe *et. al.* 2011).

With only a few years left to achieve Botswana's Vision 2016, the country is unlikely to reach some of its goals. In particular, goals envisaging a prosperous and democratic nation are under threat. The 2011 annual Vision 2016 awards were dominated by just one pillar of the vision, that of 'A compassionate, just and caring nation', and there were no nominees in the category of 'An open, democratic and accountable nation' (Keoreng 2011). The nominations were made by members of the public in a radio phone-in programme, as well as via self-nomination. There are various possible reasons for the public's failure to point to deserving individuals or institutions, but it appears to reflect the underutilisation of democracy by the people of Botswana. This view is contradicted, however, by the results of the Afrobarometer survey of 2008 (University of Botswana Faculty 2008). The report documents that 91% of people polled were satisfied with the country's democracy, with 56% regarding Botswana as a full democracy. A more plausible possibility is that the people of Botswana could have bought into President Ian Khama's dismissal of politics as 'dirty' (Burgis 2009).

Another indicator that could be helpful in diagnosing Botswana's democracy is the state of its democratic institutions, both statutory and non-statutory. Those that are supposed to be directly linked to human rights, such as the Office of the Ombudsman and the Intelligence Security Tribunal, are either handicapped by their organisational structures, as is the former (Ombudsman 2008), or entirely handpicked by the president without any effective oversight, such as the latter. The Ombudsman's report of 2004 decried the fact that it could not be referred directly to parliament, but had to be submitted to the president. This reporting line has, in the past, compromised the role of the Ombudsman. A case in point involved the use of the State helicopter by the then vice-president, Lieutenant Ian Khama. The opposition Botswana Congress Party (BCP) reported the matter to the Ombudsman, who ruled in its favour. Then president Festus Mogae used his presidential powers to dismiss the case, saying the vice-president was permitted by him to use the aircraft. A similarly dismissive attitude has also been evident when the president has been involved in the selection of officers to lead critical bodies such as the Tribunal on the Directorate of Intelligence and Security. The president appointed people very close to him, including a relative, Tsetsele Fantan, and an active member of the ruling party, Isaac Seloko (Anon. n.d.a).

A question that arises, therefore, could be: Has Botswana's democracy and human rights performance progressed, declined or stagnated over time? To help us find an answer, this chapter will look at whether existing laws, institutions and governance practices are consistent with democracy as understood universally. To what extent has the absence of certain laws and democratic institutions or practices affected the country's progress?

CIVIL AND POLITICAL RIGHTS

The people of Botswana are able to approach the courts to demand protection when their civil and political rights are threatened. There has been a gradual upsurge of court cases involving individuals and governing authorities in the country. The establishment of the Directorate of Intelligence and Security Services (DISS) saw an increase in accusations of spying against the State. The protection of civil rights was also tested in court cases involving complaints against traditional practices in the Kgatleng district. A number of individuals took the traditional leadership to court for alleged illegal floggings by the royal regiments.

65. **How free are all people from intimidation and fear, physical violation against their person, arbitrary arrest and detention?** (5)

Personal freedoms are guaranteed in S3 of the Botswana Constitution, which provides explicitly that no person living in the country shall have his or her freedoms violated (ROB 1997:S3). There are generally fewer incidents of personal violation, although concerns are being expressed more vocally. The 2009 African Media Barometer reported a lot of fear among citizens, with people increasingly looking over their shoulders in their various activities or conversations (MISA 2009a). Trade unions and opposition parties have been complaining about phone tapping by government security agents, something that the government denies. In fact, the president has denied allegations that he used the spy unit DISS to eavesdrop on the opposition (Anon. n.d.b). The government denial is, however, not helped by a High Court case in which a former deputy army commander, Major-General Pius Mokgware, sued the Botswana Telecommunications Corporation for allegedly facilitating the bugging of his phone (Piet 2011a). This case confirmed that the fear of a watchful 'Big Brother' was real. In another case, a spy equipment supplier, Dukef Holdings, went to court to sue the Botswana police for breach of contract after the government allegedly failed to pay for the supply of the equipment as allegedly agreed. The matter was settled out of court (Morewagae 2011c).

The DISS in particular has come under serious public attack, accused of underhand tactics. The director-general, Isaac Kgosi, has repeatedly denied the allegations (Gabz FM

News 2011). The accusations are not abating, however, and Kgosi has been heard on radio boasting about knowing a political party that supported research by the Centre for Strategic and International Studies whose report came down hard on the DISS itself (Mosikare 2011).

Of particular concern regarding the security of individuals is that, in 2009, there was a reported rise in extrajudicial killings by the State security forces. According to media reports, a number of crime suspects were shot by the security forces, of whom 11 died. Most of the victims had apparently been fleeing or resisting arrest. Some of the cases were found to be lawful killings and closed, while others proceeded to prosecution (Bureau of Democracy, Human Rights, and Labour 2010). The concerns and rumours were validated by the court case in 2011 in which four army members were convicted for executing John Kalafatis. They were all given custodial sentences and only one successfully applied for bail pending appeal as at the end of 2011 (Anon. n.d.c). These atrocities attracted criticism from civil society, including the Law Society of Botswana, which condemned the killings and threatened to take the president and government to the International Criminal Court (ICC) if such incidents persisted (Anon. 2009).

In 2009, at the height of the problem, the vice-president of the Republic of Botswana, Mompati Merafhe, was said to have undermined the seriousness of the problem, stating that 'one or two killings' should not raise such alarm nor taint the country's image. The opposition parties, in particular, condemned him and raised the issue when he received the 'world citizen award' (Makgapha 2011). Reports of such incidents came to a sudden end at the close of 2009, after a public outcry as well as threats to report President Ian Khama to the ICC.

Botswana continues to allow cultural practices deemed inhuman and undemocratic in the context of the Universal Declaration on Human Rights (UDHR). The customary court system, although lauded for its efficiency and affordability, has come under attack, especially from legal practitioners, for not allowing legal representation in its hearings. Section 28 of Botswana's Penal Code allows corporal punishment, which is commonly meted out by the customary courts. A lawsuit reached the courts over the death of 15-year-old Biki Kalodi, who died a week after he was flogged at the customary court (Modikwa 2011). According to media reports, Kalodi died following four strokes at the local *kgotla* (customary court) administered as punishment for slapping another boy. A similar case was reported in the media when a young lady, Dineo Mooketsi, lost her pregnancy after some regiments in the Kgatleng district allegedly whipped her and her partner, Simon Molwane. In her fifth month of pregnancy, she was allegedly given six lashes and her boyfriend ten strokes by a regiment of Bakgatla tribesmen (Baaitse 2010).

These cases signify the existence of similar incidents that go unreported across the country and could well influence a call for review of corporal punishment, both at schools and in the customary courts. The protests have reached the African Commission on Human and Peoples' Rights, which, on 2 March 2005, called on the Botswana government to 'end its enforcement of the inhuman and degrading corporal punishment'. It also advised that alternatives to corporal punishment, such as community service, should be considered.[1]

While this practice has been tolerated for a long time across the country, it has recently come under concentrated focus following its widely reported use in the Kgatleng area, especially after the enthronement of Kgosi Kgafela Kgafela. The *kgosi* himself faces legal charges relating to allegations of unlawful floggings by his regiments.

66. To what extent are people able to protect themselves against discriminatory treatment by the State? (4)

The absence of oversight institutions dedicated to the protection and enforcement of human rights weakens efforts to reduce excesses by the State. One of the significant stumbling blocks obstructing the enjoyment of rights in the country relates to access to the courts. For example, of the 13 reported cases of shooting by State operatives in the past three years, only a few reached the courts through a partly pro bono process. This could indicate resource constraints impairing the ability of citizens to take such matters to court. A positive step could be the establishment of a publicly controlled police tribunal to speed up the processing of allegations of police torture and other misdeeds. The Member of Parliament (MP) for Lobatse, Nehemiah Modubule, has already notified parliament of his intentions to call for such a body. Currently complainants against the State or authorities have to wait for the normal pace of procedures in the regular courts.

A key issue in the country is the State's neglect of indigenous languages. Although Setswana activists call for greater empowerment of the language, it at least enjoys recognition as the national language, unlike others. Rantao (2009) observes that by being identified as subordinate, these minority languages are 'denied the right to permeate the structures of linguistic cultural development at the national level, so that they cannot reflect their own cultural values and prescription in language form at the national cultural levels'.

The Constitution of Botswana recognises by name eight Setswana-speaking tribes: Bakwena, Bangwaketse, Bakgatla, Batawana, Bangwato, Balete, Batlokwa and Barolong (Moumakwa 2011). The amendment of the Constitution in 2006 did not help much in ameliorating superiority and inferiority issues, as there still remain two parallel processes of appointing members of the House of Chiefs, one for the paramount chiefs (major tribes) and another for the marginal tribes.

Botswana laws criminalise sodomy. This has come to be loosely interpreted as criminalising gays and lesbianism or same-sex relationships. It is generally believed that such relationships are illegal, although this is not necessarily the case. A group representing gays and lesbians (LeGaBiBo, or Lesbians, Gays and Bisexuals of Botswana) was denied registration by the State and had to rely on the goodwill of other rights organisations to take its messages forward (BONELA & LeGaBiBo 2008). The mere fact of denying registration means that the gay movement is unable to fight for its rights as that would be considered illegal. This means that gay people have great difficulty claiming services that could expose their sexual orientation. For instance, when people have contracted sexually transmitted infections in Botswana, they are usually asked to bring their partners when seeking treatment. However, if same-sex partnerships are illegal, such people are unlikely to expose themselves to health personnel, because they fear being brought to the attention of the law enforcement authorities.

67. To what extent are people able to use the legal system to protect their person and property against the State? (6)

The Constitution of Botswana, in Chapter 2, protects people from being deprived of their property without compensation. A well-known case of an individual taking the government to task to claim her rights is that of Unity Dow, who successfully changed the citizenship law that had initially denied children the right to adopt their mother's citizenship where the father was not a Botswana citizen.

Another illustration involved the Basarwa people challenging the State over their occupation of the Central Kalahari Game Reserve. On 13 December 2006 the court affirmed their right to live in the reserve.[2] This case, heard by the three judges Maruping Dibotelo, Mphathi Phumaphi and Unity Dow, proved that the people could use the courts to claim back their rights.

There have also been a number of recent successful lawsuits against the State. People are using their right to sue the State for negligence or illegal detention. A case in point is that of a mother whose baby was stillborn as a result of negligence on the part of health personnel. The court ordered that the mother be compensated to the amount of 250 000 Pula. Another is of a prominent politician, David Tawele, who successfully sued the State for wrongful detention (Kgalemang 2011).

The law is not completely protective of citizens, however. The case between the former secretary-general of the ruling BDP, Gomolemo Motswaledi, and the president of Botswana showed that the latter could easily take advantage of the law and not account for some of his actions. The immunity afforded by the Constitution to a sitting president, at least in the interpretation of both the High Court and the Court of Appeal, was an eye-opener to many people. The judges did not hear the merits of the case, but only attended to the interpretation of S41 of the Constitution, which provided immunity to the president.

The legal protection of statutes has also proven to be vulnerable to the dictates of the ruling elites, as illustrated by the sudden change in classification of the teaching service and other trades to prevent practitioners of those trades from joining in mainstream industrial action (ROB 2004). After the public service strike, the ruling party used its majority in parliament to amend the Trade Disputes Act (2004) and categorise teaching and veterinary services, among others, as essential. This is despite the fact that Botswana has ratified International Labour Organisation (ILO) conventions No. 87 and 98, whose definition of essential services, unions insist, does not to apply to these particular professions.[3]

In their court affidavits, the unions argued: 'These conventions, have been interpreted by the ILO Committee of Experts, human rights tribunals, distinguished courts the world over, and eminent jurists, as requiring that the classification of essential services be limited to those services the interruption of which would endanger the health, the lives or the personal safety of the whole population' (Morewagae 2011a).

The unions further claimed lack of consultation during the sudden change of the Trade Disputes Act (2004). Changing laws or creating new ones to suit individual or partisan interests is uncharacteristic of a republic that abides by the rule of law. It further reduces people's confidence in the rule of law.

The ratification of international agreements is also a matter of concern. The non-ratification of conventions could deny citizens the opportunity to take their government to task when violations are suspected. International human rights organisations such as Amnesty International have voiced their concern to the government of Botswana. In particular, Amnesty International opposed Botswana's membership of the United Nations Human Rights Council at the elections scheduled for 20 May 2011.

Amnesty International raised questions about Botswana's commitment to the ratification of the following international human rights instruments: the Optional Protocol to the Convention Against Torture and Other Cruel, Inhuman, Degrading Treatment or Punishment; the International Convention for the Protection of All Persons from Enforced Disappearance; the Convention on the Rights of Persons with Disabilities and its optional protocol; and the International Convention on the Protection of the Rights of all Migrant Workers (Balule & Maripe 2000).

68. How effective is the protection of the freedoms of expression, information and assembly for all persons irrespective of their social grouping? (4)

The Constitution's recognition of freedom of expression and its sister freedoms is compromised by a number of legal instruments, as well as the absence of transparency laws to protect whistle-blowers, ensure access to information and oblige public figures to declare their assets and liabilities. The existence of immigration laws, the National Security Act (1986), the Media Practitioners Act (2009), the Cinematograph Act (1972) and several other restrictive policies have meant less enjoyment of freedom of expression.[4]

Immigration law has been used to invoke presidential powers declaring foreigners prohibited immigrants. Both the victims and the public are denied the reasons for such deportations as the president is not obliged to divulge them. The secrecy involved in these processes always attracts criticism and allegations of misuse of power by the president (MISA 2009b). Professor Kenneth Good, formerly of the University of Botswana, was deported under such circumstances. Other deportees include journalists and human rights activists. Speculation has been rife that they were deported because their views showed the government in a bad light (MISA 2010). Using the same immigration laws, the government in 2007 banned several human rights activists and journalists from entering the country without first applying for visas. This was despite the fact that they were from countries that have no visa requirement for entering Botswana (MISA 2007).

What are generally referred to as 'insult laws' are also seen as inhibitors of freedom of expression (Balule & Maripe 2000). Insult laws are found in the Penal Code and are used to prosecute people for saying unfavourable things about the president and other national symbols. Section 91 of the Code states:

any person who does any act or utters any words or publishes any writing with intent to insult or to bring into contempt or ridicule –

(a) the Arms or Ensigns Armorial of Botswana

(b) the National Flag of Botswana

(c) the Standard of the President of Botswana

(d) the National Anthem of Botswana

is guilty of an offence and liable to a fine not exceeding P500 (ROB 1964:S91).

A case in point was that of a foreigner who was deported for apparently referring to the president when he was quarrelling with his employees, and another was that of a South African, Dorsey Dube, who was detained for saying the president looked like a Mosarwa (Bushman) (Survival International n.d.).

FREEDOM OF ASSOCIATION AND PARTICIPATION

69. How secure is the freedom for all to practise their own religion, language and culture?   (3)

There are no known obstacles to practising one's religion of choice in Botswana. However, the Apostolic Faith, whose members are also known as the Zezurus, often clash with the law on a number of issues. The most common is their refusal to participate in medical vaccination campaigns and mainstream schooling, citing their religious beliefs. In such cases the government uses Botswana's laws to ensure that children are not denied their right to life or education (ROB 2009).

The Evangelical Fellowship of Botswana had to seek the intervention of the High Court in order to practise their faith in Mochudi after they were allegedly harassed and barred from worshipping by the local royal authority. The court ruled in favour of the church, ordering that they were free to worship anywhere in Botswana.[5]

A related issue is that of language and culture. In Botswana, there are many languages and cultures, although most are not immediately apparent. Many observers believe that this is the result of a deliberate policy of creating a united nation. Godfrey Mwakikagile (2009:110) observes that Botswana is a 'heterogeneous society' and not the 'homogeneous society the government is trying to build'.

While the Constitution states very clearly that discrimination of whatever kind is not tolerated, it takes away that right by giving parallel recognition to membership of *Ntlo ya Dikgosi*, or the House of Chiefs (ROB 1997:S77–85). Only Setswana and English are regarded as national and official languages respectively.

According to former president Masire, it was a deliberate decision to assimilate all other tribal identities under the Botswana nomenclature (Masire & Lewis 2006). It then followed that the national language was Setswana, and the rest were relegated to a lower status. While the intention of building a nation was good and admirable, efforts could have been made to offer some form of survival platform for other languages, without necessarily reducing the status of the national language. Setswana could still have played the unifying role, in concert with a deliberate policy to revive and promote the use of the other indigenous languages. Despite this non-recognition, speakers of some languages, such as Kalanga, were organised and, as a result, continued to demand recognition. The country's language policy has also been attacked by academics and activists (Moeng 2011).

70. To what extent do people feel free to associate with others in order to influence government? To what extent does government action encourage or discourage people to associate with others in order to influence government? (4)

71. To what extent do people organise themselves into associations in order to influence government and to what extent are the associations of civil society independent of government? (4)

72. How far do women participate in political and public life at all levels? (6)

There are many registered civil society organisations in Botswana. The Societies Act (1972) regulates the registration of associations and societies. There has been vibrant advocacy in areas such as HIV/Aids, the media and human rights, particularly at the level of community-based organisations. Organisations including the Botswana Council of Non-Governmental Organisations (BOCONGO), the Media Institute of Southern Africa (MISA), Ditshwanelo, the Botswana Network on Ethics, Law and HIV/Aids (BONELA), the Botswana Christian Council and Emang Basadi have focused on lobbying, individually and collectively, for policy changes around human rights matters. Their collective effort, in conjunction with trade unions such as the Botswana Sector of Educators Trade Union, was more visible in their campaign under the umbrella of the Botswana Civil Society Solidarity Coalition for Zimbabwe, which contributed to shaping Botswana's response to Zimbabwe's political unrest. The Coalition for Freedom of Expression was another formation that brought organisations together around a single issue.

However, although freedom of association is recognised in the Constitution, several incidents and actions have compromised that freedom. In September 2011 the government ordered public service workers to boycott an awards ceremony organised by MISA Botswana. The statement read:

As the government of Botswana does not accept the legitimacy of said awards, we are hereby instructing that under no circumstance should any government public relations officer attend said ceremony, or otherwise accept any resulting award or undertake any other action that would associate government with said ceremony. Put simply we expect all public officers to boycott this event.

The government spokesperson, Dr Jeff Ramsay, warned civil servants against attending the awards, accusing the institute of having made political statements during the previous awards (Gabz FM 96.2 2011). The government's responses in its relations with MISA Botswana bring to attention the government's views on those that hold different opinions and could result in self-censorship by civil society organisations.

Botswana is reputed to have done exceptionally well on issues of gender parity in primary and secondary schools. According to the Botswana Millennium Development Goals status report of 2010, there has been considerable growth in women's participation in decision-making positions in both public and business sectors. The same status report observes that there has been a significant improvement in the formulation of policy and laws that ensure some balance between men and women (ROB & UN 2010).

Conversely, Botswana is one of only two countries in the Southern African Development Community (SADC) that have not signed the SADC Gender and Development Protocol. This has caused some unease among the gender movement and questions the country's commitment on the issue. Civil society organisations, among them BOCONGO, Gender Links and Emang Basadi, have collectively tried to lobby the government into signing, but in vain. This is not helped by the fact that the country is still lagging behind in the political representation of women in parliament and Cabinet, as it has not achieved the 30% quota set by the SADC.

73. How free from harassment and intimidation are individuals and groups working to protect human rights? (5)

There are several civil society organisations dedicated to monitoring human rights in the country.[6] The Centre for Human Rights, Ditshwanelo, is most notable as an all-embracing human rights organisation, while there are other sectoral ones such as MISA, BONELA and the trade unions. While in the past there were never reported cases of harassment and intimidation by the State, of late the government has shown some discomfort with certain organisations and individuals. The decision by the government to ban public service workers from attending MISA activities could be viewed as harassment and intimidation. The government also recently accused BONELA of disturbing HIV/Aids commemorations simply because they circulated their advocacy pamphlet at the event in Moshupa (Ontebetse n.d.).

Journalists have reported unlawful detention and destruction of their equipment by the police. MISA Botswana reported at least two incidents when the police prevented journalists from covering activities and destroyed their film and memory cards. A photojournalist, Lefoko Mogapaesi, was detained after he allegedly refused to leave a Magistrate's Court in a particular restricted area during the trial of a local chief. He was kept in detention for some hours before MISA Botswana successfully negotiated his release (MISA 2010).

During the two-month-long public service strike, from April to July 2011, the unions and political parties were denied permits for some of their intended marches. Permits to march or gather in a public place have to be applied for in writing at a police station. Information to be submitted includes the time and date, the place and the period for which the event is planned to take place.[7] However, sometimes it is not as easy as it appears, especially when the reason for the march or meeting is to protest something that the government might regard as sensitive. The police sometimes refuse permits under the pretext that they do not have enough resources to provide escorts or because of circumstances beyond their control (Botswana Congress Party 2011). The unions were faced with rejections when they resolved to stage marches to constituency MPs at their constituency offices. Another intended petition targeted the chiefs or *dikgosi* at their wards. The Minister of Local Government,

Lebonaamang Mokalake, wrote to *dikgosi*, ordering them to reject the unions' petitions.[8] This led to some traditional leaders refusing to abide by the government instructions and instead welcoming the workers' petitions. Where *dikgosi* complied with the minister, the union members were ordered not to march. In Moshupa, the unionists tried to march, but were prevented by the police.

During the strike, however, the police on the whole demonstrated calmness, even in response to open provocation. They generally avoided using excessive force, preferring to detain offenders briefly instead. *The Telegraph* published a photograph of a policeman taking cover with one of the students in the middle of riots in Molepolole. The unfortunate thing is that, in some cases, the detainees allegedly included under-age students.[9]

POLITICAL PARTIES

74. How freely are political parties able to form, recruit members and engage with the public? (7)

75. How free are opposition or non-governing parties to organise within the legislature and outside of it? (6)

In Botswana it is easy to form a political party. There is no restriction on the number of members. This does not mean, however, that everything is plain sailing: the ruling party has used its incumbency to reject several electoral reforms that opposition parties have called for (Molomo 1998). Among the reforms the parties have called for is State funding for all those participating in the elections. The supporters of State funding of political parties have argued that it is in the public interest for political parties to be assisted in their participation. They have further argued that the ruling party enjoys the advantage of State resources at the expense of other competing players – for example, the use of State helicopters by the president and vice-president during political campaigns. The ruling party claims this all comes with incumbency and there is not much it can do. Some observers, however, continue to point out the importance of funding political parties. To illustrate this, Professor Molomo maintains that opposition parties lack even the most basic needs.

To be effective, political parties need funds to finance their campaigns, to print campaign materials, billboards, fliers, as well as to advertise in the electronic and print media. Opposition parties have fared poorly in this regard (BOPA News 2000).

76. How fair and effective are the rules governing party discipline in the legislature and within the party? (6)

77. How far are parties effective membership organisations, and how far are members able to influence party policy? Are all individual members privy to sufficient information about their party, including details of private donors? (5)

78. To what extent are political parties able to aggregate the interest of all social groups? (5)

There has been concern regarding internal party democracy in Botswana, notably within the ruling BDP, the Botswana National Front (BNF), the BCP and the Botswana Movement for Democracy (BMD). The BMD, a splinter party of the BDP, cited lack of internal party democracy when its members decamped in March 2010. The same reason was given when the BCP left the leading opposition party, the BNF, in 1998. In both cases the splinter parties had issues with the presidents of their original parties. It appears that parties generally, to varying degrees, find it very difficult to manage their internal challenges, especially when it comes to leadership contestation and enforcing discipline. This was clear during the BDP split, when the former secretary-general sought the intervention of the law to contest his expulsion. In an indictment on the Constitution, the court used S41, which gives the president immunity, and the case was dismissed with costs.[10]

The subsequent Mahalapye BDP congress after the split was squeezed into one day, to suit the president's preference. This was a departure from the usual three to four days. The president's imposed list, otherwise known as the 'compromise list', was endorsed by the congress to become the next central committee.

The opposition parties cannot claim innocence in matters of internal democracy. The BCP's non-contested elections, especially for key positions, cannot be said to be in the interests of democracy, while the BNF's appetite for suspending and expelling dissenting members has stifled participatory democracy in the party. Parliament has come up with standing orders that are generally seen as an improvement on the previous ones. One of the key improvements is the procedure for tabling a private member's Bill, which now allows members to bring Bills without first having to get the blessing of parliament.

As for the aggregation of interest of various social groupings, the parties do have internal sub-groups, such as women's and youth leagues, but questions could be raised about the effectiveness of these groupings. The BDP has the most submissive youth league, whose voice is rarely heard on national issues. In those cases when such organs are more audible, such as in the BNF, the result is usually a collision with the leadership of the party. The women's leagues are the most silent organs of the political parties, save for their involvement in fundraising and campaigning for their male counterparts. Their subordinate character has made them almost insignificant in the decision-making processes of their organisations, which could partly explain the fact that there is little or no representation of women in any political structure in the country.

The low participation of party members in party structures, apart from the central committees, has seriously compromised their involvement. In all parties most decisions are centralised, leaving very little space for participation by other structures. This was most evident in the opposition parties' cooperation talks, for which party members gave the central committees blanket negotiating mandates. Policy formulation for the envisaged umbrella party was left to a few individuals whose work was never brought before the wider membership.

MEDIA RIGHTS

79. To what extent does the legal system ensure that print and electronic media are free to print or say what they want about those in power in both government and the private sector? (5)

80. To what extent are people and organisations able to disseminate their views via print or electronic media? (7)

81. To what extent are the print and electronic media independent from government? How pluralistic is the ownership of print and electronic media? (5)

The media in Botswana are relatively vibrant. They have shown their tenacity in pursuit of corruption stories. For a long time the media environment has been described as free, without persecution of journalists. The latest indices, however, are starting to qualify this freedom of the press, especially since the enactment of the Media Practitioners Act (2009). Freedom House, in its 2011 index, described Botswana's media freedom as partly free as opposed to free.[11]

The decline has been gradual. The government's impatience and eagerness to control the independent media have been quite open. For example, the ruling party wrote a letter to Gabz FM in 2008 that accused the radio presenters of 'fomenting hate, mistrust, chaos and disharmony amongst your listeners against the president'.[12]

The effect of such intervention by the ruling party, well founded or not, is a loss of editorial independence and an escalation of self-censorship. In 2002, the government lost a court case after it had instructed its departments and parastatals not to place advertisements in the *Botswana Guardian* and the *Midweek Sun*. The fallout came after the paper had run some negative stories about then president, Festus Mogae. Justice Lesetedi ruled that the government decision was unconstitutional as it was intended to influence 'the newspapers to change their editorial policy' (IFEX 2001).

Another threat to press freedom in Botswana is the participation of the State in media ownership and editorial activities. The private media and media activists have complained about the commercialisation of the State's *Daily News* and its radio station, RB2 (UN 2007), the argument being that such a move is meant to deny private media business in an already limited market.

The private press enjoys more independence than any other media, thanks to the easy registration of newspapers without interference from the government. Although there are some administrative requirements for registration, the process has always been straightforward.

However, only a few newspapers survive. The print industry is self-selecting as it is solely dependent on the market. The failure of most players can be attributed to various factors, including the monopolistic nature of the old establishment and a private sector too small to supply sufficient advertising revenue.

Broadcasting, the most popular medium, does not enjoy the same independence as the printed media, and is mainly controlled by the State. The State issues licences for private broadcasters and owns a national television and two radio channels, while there are three private radio stations.[13] The process of awarding licences is usually slow and there is no clear indication of when applications are open.

Self-censorship is more apparent at private radio stations as they fear having their licences revoked. In 2009, Gabz FM banned political reporting after being intimidated by the publicity committee of the BDP.[14] Duma FM fired some of its presenters after allegations of intimidation from a political party (MISA 2009b). The journalists had presented a programme in which listeners had the opportunity to complain about political parties, especially the ruling party.

The government of Botswana enacted the Media Practitioners Act (2009), a law that regulates the media. The media in Botswana had resisted this law in its varying versions since 1997, when it was first initiated.

The major contentious areas are the registration and accreditation of journalists, the fines and jail term prescribed for offending publishers, the political involvement in the appointment of complaints and appeals committees, the minister's power to dissolve the media council, and the prescriptive nature of the right to reply.

Media activists believe that these areas are only there to ensure control of the private media. They argue that the law is unconstitutional and hope that the courts will declare it invalid (MISA/IFEX 2009).

The Code of Conduct for Broadcasters During Elections, compiled by the National Broadcasting Board, has a number of clauses that limit free broadcasting during elections. The code, introduced before the 2009 elections, controls the conduct of broadcasters during the election period. Some of its limitations include a ban on political advertisements and limiting political broadcasts to a period not exceeding two months before the elections.

While this is well intended and designed to balance coverage, it is in effect an inhibition of freedom of expression. The good side of this regulation is that it prevents those with money from splashing it around randomly, disadvantaging those without, but in Botswana's case such regulations come too late, when the ruling party has dominated the State airwaves for the preceding five years.

State media journalists are regulated by the Public Service Act (2008), and because of the Act's restrictions on access to information, their journalistic work is heavily compromised (ROB 2008b). In fact it has been government policy since the early days of State media that government journalists are merely recorders of government information and are not expected to 'editorialise' about it (Masire & Lewis 2006). It is because of this foundation that State media continue to endure political interference from the ruling party.

Control of the State media, which enjoy the widest reach in the country, was moved into the Office of the President after the 2009 elections (MISA 2010). This ensured the president direct control over the most prestigious political tool.

The State media were subjected to unprecedented civil society criticism over their coverage of the public service workers' strike, which was generally viewed as government propaganda. During the two-month period of the strike, State television only covered the president's reactions and completely ignored the side of the workers. Even this created problems for the government, as it gave contradictory statements along the way. At one point the Minister of Health, Dr John Seakgosing, was on the screen assuring the nation that the health sector was not affected, but the story changed when the government had to rush to court to demand the return of nurses.

82. To what extent do citizens have equal access to adequate information, including news and other media?   (2)

The Constitution of Botswana guarantees freedom of information in S12, which states that every citizen has the freedom to receive ideas and information without interference. While this may seem adequate, it falls short of guaranteeing access to information. In other words, the people of Botswana have the right to receive information, but the right of access is not explicitly assured. For instance, if a custodian of information does not proactively give that information out, can the Constitution help one demand access? Without a proper law providing for access to information, such a custodian might have room to manoeuvre, and to pick and choose which information to release, without any guiding instrument.

MISA conducted two surveys in 2010 and 2011 to find out if the country was open enough, and both times the government failed the test (Mogapi 2011). In the first survey the situation was better, as there was a winner in the open government category, but in 2011 no government department responded to MISA's requests for information (Mogapi 2011).

Through the document that set out Vision 2016, the people of Botswana expressed the need for a freedom of information Act (Presidential Task Group 1997). The same sentiments are expressed in the Ombudsman's annual report for 2008. A Commonwealth expert has suggested, however, that the prospective legislation be called an access to information Act instead of a freedom of information Act.[15] This suggestion makes sense since one may argue that freedom of information is already given in the Constitution, while it is access that the nation and activists are yearning for.

This law could also have some positive implications on the issuance of a writ of elections and other electoral processes, whose transparency is vital to safeguard the country's political stability. Currently only the president knows the election date, yet details of this kind are generally regarded as public information, and an access to information Act may be used to demand them.

The debates in the parliament of Botswana are currently not broadcast live for the public's direct access, although the transcript can be read later in *Hansard*. This denies the people the opportunity to follow the proceedings of parliament as it is impossible for everyone to attend in person. As a result, voters go to the elections without a proper appreciation of the issues, especially when such information is not derived directly from parliamentarians. Legislators themselves have raised the issue, complaining that State reporters misinterpreted their deliberations and expressing their desire to be heard directly.

The secretiveness of the government and its leaders is often unnecessary and, in some cases, illegal. The 'Green Book', which is officially titled *President, the Vice President, Minister, Speaker, Assistant Minister, Deputy Speaker and Leader of the Opposition: Function, Pay and Privileges*, is not made available to the public despite the explicit note that it should at least be sold (Maundeni (ed.) 2008).

Following the national strike of 2011, the government demanded that public servants be sworn to silence on information they came across in their work. While this practice was initially confined to managerial positions, now it is forced on every government employee. Trade unions protested and even called on their members to ignore the instruction.

CONCLUSION

The Constitution of the Republic of Botswana needs to be assessed with a view to making it more democratic. The Constitution as it is now falls short of modern constitutions that have taken a step forward in recognising freedoms beyond just natural rights. A Bill of Rights including second-generation rights would provide a link between the people and the Constitution.

Traditional leaders, notably Kgosi Kgafela of Bakgatla, have expressed their disapproval of the Constitution. They protest at the diminished status of *dikgosi* in running the affairs of the country.

The weaknesses of the Constitution were exposed when, subsequent to the opening of the February 2012 parliamentary session, the house was left without a leader of the opposition, as the standing orders could not provide sufficient guidance on procedures when opposition parties wrangle over the position.

Botswana needs transparency laws that open up the government and provide access to socio-economic opportunities, because the people's access to services is compromised by their lack of knowledge. Currently, the country does not have legislation governing access to information, the declaration of assets and liabilities, or the protection of whistle-blowers. Under such a closed government, people are unable to enjoy their rights and freedoms fully. The absence of community radio means people in areas remote from urban centres cannot access media to enjoy the opportunities that come with such resources.

Political democracy at national level usually succeeds if it is well established at the level of individual parties. There is therefore a need to strengthen democracy within parties, because it is noticeably deficient in all Botswana's political parties. Without fully enjoying democracy in their parties, people are unlikely to notice declining trends of democracy in the national body politic. While it is true that special focus should be placed on the current ruling party, it must not be forgotten that opposition parties are contenders for that position and, as such, their neglect of democratic norms is as deserving of disapproval from the public.

The country is fortunate enough to have had a culture of political stability and tolerance. The need now is to take advantage of this situation and improve on the quality of democracy and human rights. The spirit of consultation needs to be prioritised and effectively applied, and this must go beyond mere involvement. The people of Botswana have long had *therisanyo* (consultation) as one of the four recognised national principles, the others being unity, independence and self-reliance. Structures that were initially set up for this purpose, such as parliament, village development committees, parent-teacher associations and *Ntlo ya Dikgosi* (the House of Chiefs), as well as various other institutions including non-governmental organisations (NGOs), need to be strengthened and, in some cases, revived.

Reforms that need to be adopted include the funding of political parties and civil society, in particular NGOs. Funding such formations will go a long way towards protecting the security of the country as well as empowering ordinary citizens who are at present unable to access the mainstream of socio-economic and political wealth.

Various stakeholders have indicated the need for human rights in the country to be independently monitored. Currently people have to report lapses of State institutions to the very same State. This compromises the core functions of institutions such as the police, in that they have to play multiple roles of governance. Botswana does not have a human rights commission, and this lack is a serious indictment on Botswana's human rights, because it denies the country the ability to monitor its human rights situation in a way that could win the confidence of the people. Such a body would advise the government and create awareness among the public of human rights issues.

The death penalty remains on Botswana's statutes. Human rights pressure groups such as Ditshwanelo continue to ask for its abolition, or at least some form of moratorium. Their latest call was in February 2012, following the hanging of convicted murderer, Zibane Thamo, on 31 January 2012.

Some urgent measures need to be taken to restore respect for the State's security organs. The DISS, for instance, needs to be repackaged to deal with the negative perception that has stalked it since inception. Just as South Africa did with its Directorate of Special Operations (known as the Scorpions), albeit with different motivation, Botswana may have to overhaul its security organs with a view to improving their effectiveness and acceptance in society.

It is also necessary for the government to look at international conventions and agreements that it has not yet signed or ratified, with a view to doing so. The country cannot operate effectively in isolation from the international community. Some of the unsigned instruments are highly relevant to the successful recognition of human rights and democracy. Among these are the SADC Protocol on Gender and Development and the African Charter on Democracy, Elections and Governance.

Botswana must also give Vision 2016 some sincere attention. The government does not seem to have internalised the principles set out the document (Presidential Task Group 1997), save for the pillar of a compassionate nation. The document contains universally accepted reference points for a sound democracy that could help the country improve its democratic credentials.

Finally, while it is true that the Constitution of the country needs to be reviewed, the role of cultural practices and norms must be carefully assessed to avoid a re-emergence of tribal dictatorships. The current Constitution must be the baseline for the future aspirations of the people of Botswana.

ENDNOTES

1 African Commission on Human and Peoples' Rights.

2 http://www.ditshwanelo.org.bw/ethnic.html.

3 ILO, Convention No. 87: Convention Concerning Freedom of Association and Protection of the Right to Organise. Available: http://bit.ly/GRPKfT; ILO, Convention 98: Convention Concerning the Application of the Principles of the Right to Organise and to Bargain Collectively. Available: http://bit.ly/GSSSJ8.

4 *Good v State, Clay v State.*

5 *Evangelical Fellowship of Botswana v Bakgatla royals.*

6 http://www.bocongo.org.bw.

7 http://www.gov.bw/en/Ministries--Authorities/Ministries/State-President/Botswana-Police-Service-/Tools-and-Services/Services--Forms/Public-Meeting-Permit/.

8 Kgosi Mosadi Seboko of Bamalete read the minister's letter at the *kgotla* while receiving the protesting workers.

9 http://www.ditshwanelo.org.bw.

10 *Motswaledi v State President*

11 'Freedom of the Press: Botswana'. Available: http://bit.ly/GRioz4.

12 Letter from BDP to Gabz FM management.

13 Yarona FM news.

14 Gabz FM management letter to staff.

15 Commonwealth Experts Report on Botswana Freedom of Information Act.

SECTION FIVE

HUMAN DIGNITY
AND DEMOCRACY

BY ALICE MOGWE & INGRID MELVILLE

'Democracy' is generally defined as a form of government in which all adult citizens have an equal say in the decisions that affect their lives. A basic feature of democracy is the capacity of individuals to participate freely and fully in the life of their society. In order to apply the twofold test of democracy – 'firstly, do the people rule, and secondly, do the people rule equally?' (Chanza & Sylvester 2010:257) – one has to examine the form of democracy that prevails in Botswana and the context within which it operates.

Democracy represents a value system and development of democracy in Botswana has been guided by the national principles of democracy, development, self-reliance, unity and *botho*[1] since the country's independence in 1966. The framework is laid out in the Constitution of 1965. However, Botswana's democracy cannot be looked at only within the confines of the Constitution. According to several academics, including Dr Gloria Somolekae, former lecturer at the University of Botswana and now Assistant Minister of Finance and

Developmental Planning, '[m]any researchers today have come to appreciate the fact that the notion of democracy does not lack roots in Africa. Therefore any effort which is aimed at understanding the process of democratisation should not start at independence as customarily is the case' (Somolekae 2008:4). An assessment of democracy in Botswana should take into consideration the procedural and institutional framework for democracy characterised by the provisions of the Constitution, and the lived experiences of the people in Botswana, which are guided by practices and customs.

Democracy can be seen as providing an enabling framework for the population to thrive. The country is often considered to be a shining light of democracy in Africa, despite the fact that Botswana's Constitution does not guarantee economic, social and cultural rights, and access to basic goods and services is provided largely on the basis of laws and a policy framework. Despite the absence of constitutional guarantees to entrench access to basic goods and services, the government of Botswana makes such goods and services widely available to its citizens.

Botswana is third on the 2011 Ibrahim Index of African Governance[2] and is a State party to a number of international human rights instruments that deal with economic, social and cultural rights, such as the African Charter on Human and Peoples' Rights and the Universal Declaration on Human Rights of 1948 (UDHR). However, Botswana is not a State party to the International Covenant on Economic, Social and Cultural Rights (ICESCR), and therefore has not demonstrated a binding commitment to international norms and standards that support human dignity.

It should also be noted that Botswana has a dual legal system. This means that even those international and regional human rights instruments that it has committed itself to are not enforceable in the country unless an Act of Parliament is passed that contains the principles and standards agreed to at the regional and international levels. It is only once regional and international human rights standards have been domesticated into national laws that they will be binding and applicable in Botswana.

The Constitution of Botswana, like other constitutions of the 1960s, contains only civil and political rights, also known as first-generation rights. It is silent on economic, social and cultural rights, or second-generation rights, as well as developmental and group rights, also called third-generation rights. As such, the Constitution does not provide a basis for citizens to access those basic goods and services and economic opportunities that are undoubtedly objective markers of a dignified life. While the Constitution does not impose on the government a written obligation to ensure such access to all citizens, there are laws, policies and practices that, over time, have given citizens a practical frame of reference and the expectation that the government is obliged to, and will, take the steps necessary to ensure that every citizen lives a life with dignity. While there are gaps in the national and international legislative framework to advance and safeguard the human dignity of Batswana, the national vision of Botswana, namely Vision 2016, is premised on the socio-economic advancement of citizens, as it provides a framework 'Towards prosperity for all' by 2016. The attainment of the national vision is advanced through national development plans.

In considering human dignity in Botswana, this assessment takes into consideration the statement: 'Human dignity, therefore, encapsulates the broad set of socio-economic rights of individuals that would enable them to lead dignified lives' (Chanza & Sylvester 2010:257). However, if one is to review human dignity within Botswana comprehensively, it has to be noted that culture plays a critical role in measuring the self-perceived dignity of individuals. Ethnic groupings as well as broader societal perceptions also shape the definition of human dignity. This can be linked to the assertion by Dr Somolekae that democracy in Botswana predates its independence institutions. The broader notion of human dignity as extending beyond socio-economic rights is also highlighted in the recent Court of Appeal decision in *Matsipane Mosetlhanyane and others v Attorney-General*,[3] in which the Court of Appeal made reference to the report of the United Nations (UN) Committee on Economic, Social and Cultural Rights (CESCR), although Botswana is not a State party to the ICESCR. In our view, human dignity encompasses the broad set of economic, social and cultural rights that would enable a person in Botswana to lead a dignified life. Our focus here, however, is on economic and social rights.

In this section we will cite common international indicators that demarcate the provision and protection of, and respect for, socio-economic rights such as access to health care, access to education, poverty eradication strategies, jobs and rights in the workplace, the delivery of social and economic rights, and corporate governance. We will also consider whether the absence of a constitutional framework detracts from the efficacy of the access to services and opportunities that citizens enjoy. This assessment will also consider whether the absence of constitutional protection limits the sustainability of the form of democracy in Botswana.

Due to the absence of economic, social and cultural rights in the Constitution, there is no legal indicator or guideline towards the progressive realisation of economic, social and cultural rights obligations. However, services are provided to the population.

SOCIO-ECONOMIC RIGHTS PROTECTION

83. How far are economic and social rights, including equal access to work, guaranteed for all?   (4)

84. How effectively are the basic necessities of life guaranteed, including
    a. Clean adequate and reasonably accessible water?
    b. Adequate food?
    c. Adequate housing and shelter?
    d. Adequate and unimpeded access to land?   (4)

The government's commitment to the protection of socio-economic rights is reflected in the president's State of the Nation address of 2010, in which he advocated a people-centred development approach. He stated: 'We do not want a situation in this country whereby the rich get richer and the poor get poorer. We must rather strive as a nation to try to move up the ladder of opportunity together, not leaving others behind' (Khama 2010).

Equal access to and implementation of socio-economic rights for all, including the right to work, water, food, housing, shelter and land, are not guaranteed in Botswana. At the same time, it is indisputable that the fundamental principles of human rights – the inherent dignity of human beings, equality and non-discrimination, and the indivisibility and interdependence of human rights – need to form the basis of a people-centred approach to development.

The ICESCR provides for the protection of the right to work; the right to fair conditions of employment; the right to an adequate standard of living, including the right to food, clothing and housing; the right to health; the right to education; and the right to culture. The CESCR has dealt specifically with the rights to housing (including the issue of forced evictions), food and education, the rights of persons with disabilities, and the rights of the elderly.

Because socio-economic rights are not recognised in the Constitution of Botswana, there is no entrenched obligation on the State to provide basic and essential services to the population, though international human rights law and most national rights protections are directed at the State. However, as part of its development programmes since independence in 1966, the government of Botswana has focused on the provision of infrastructure and services. These include the construction of schools, clinics and roads, as well as the provision of access to water, food (during periods of drought), education and health services.

In 2009 there was an official policy shift from poverty reduction to poverty eradication. There was a similar shift to a people-centred approach to development in 2010. The government recognises that these shifts will bring fundamentally different ways of 'doing development'. A change is needed in the paradigm of thinking, analysis and planning. Positive policy interventions by the government can result in increased access to work, water, food, housing, shelter and land, but the absence of such provisions from the Constitution means that these rights are not guaranteed for all and can become inaccessible through policy changes and legislative amendments, with no room for legal recourse by the rights holders.

Indeed, legally recognising economic, social and cultural rights is an important part of guaranteeing those rights. If rights are guaranteed through entrenched provisions in the Constitution, those clauses are, in effect, written undertakings to citizens about their rights. Variations to the written clauses are only possible after wide consultation and publicity, for instance through a national referendum. Such alterations or variations will be more easily challenged in the High Court, which is the guardian of rights. Without this constitutional recognition, the provision of services remains a response to a need and not an obligation to which the government is duty-bound. However, legal protection in itself does not guarantee access. Relevant policies and appropriate development planning, together with the legal protection of a right, are required for social, economic and cultural rights to be guaranteed.

In the recent Mosetlhanyane case,[4] the Court of Appeal noted that, in July 2010, the UN General Assembly had 'recognised the right to safe and clean drinking water as a fundamental human right that is essential for the full enjoyment of life and all human rights'. This case involved an application made by two residents of Mothomelo, a Basarwa/San community in the Central Kalahari Game Reserve. The community applied to the High Court for a declaration that they had the right to access water within the reserve. In applying the CESCR report (2003) the court noted that 'State parties should give special attention to those individuals or groups who have traditionally faced difficulties in exercising this right, including ... indigenous peoples ... States should provide resources for indigenous peoples to design, deliver and control their access to water.'

A consequence of the paradigm shift from poverty reduction to poverty eradication is that government policies and programmes need to move beyond basic needs to the attainment of acceptable levels of income. The current paradigm was premised upon the transformation of the economy through the provision of infrastructural development and ideas of trickle-down economics, according to which the State viewed its role mainly as one of 'facilitation' rather than 'intervention'. This led to the construction of roads, the delivery of health services and the building of schools and other socio-economic infrastructure.

REASONABLE ACCESS TO CLEAN AND ADEQUATE WATER

Access to safe water is a fundamental human need and, therefore, a basic human right. Contaminated water jeopardises both the physical and social health of all people. It is an affront to human dignity. (Kofi Annan, UN Secretary-General)[5]

There is no specific recognition of a right to water in international human rights instruments, including the ICESCR. However, with the increasing pressure on the world's water resources, the CESCR has begun to recognise a human right to water. It has also stated that the right to water exists as an independent right by implication from articles 11 and 12 of the ICESCR.

The Constitution of Botswana does not specifically recognise a right to water. However, as stated above, in the recent Mosetlhanyane case[6] the Court of Appeal noted that the UN General Assembly had 'recognised the right to safe and clean drinking water as a fundamental human right that is essential for the full enjoyment of life and all human rights'. The Court of Appeal also referred to the CESCR's report, which states:

Water is a limited natural resource and a public good fundamental for life and health. The human right to water is indispensable for leading a life in human dignity. It is a prerequisite for the realisation of other human rights.

It goes on:

Whereas the right to water applies to everyone, State parties should give special attention to those individuals and groups who have traditionally faced difficulties in exercising this right, including women, children, minority indigenous peoples, refugees, asylum seekers, internally displaced persons, migrant workers, prisoners and detainees.

Although Botswana is not a State party to the ICESCR, a human right to water can be inferred from the UDHR and the International Covenant on Civil and Political Rights. Botswana is a State party to both of these human rights instruments.

The water sector is governed by the Water Act (1968), the Borehole Act (1956), the Waterworks Act (1962), the Tribal Act (1968) and the National Water Supply and Sanitation Plan (1999), among other measures. Customary law recognises the availability of open water sources that may be used for domestic purposes by individuals, families and tribes.

The Water Utilities Corporation (WUC), a parastatal established in 1970 by the Water Utilities Corporation Act,[7] is responsible for potable water and waste-water service delivery. The Department of Water Affairs (DWA) in the Ministry of Minerals, Energy and Water Affairs (MMEWR) is responsible for water resources planning and management, including the construction of dams. Until May 2009, the WUC was responsible for the supply of water to towns and cities, while the DWA was responsible for the supply of bulk water to district councils and rural areas. The Water Sector Reform Project recommended the separation of water resources management from water service delivery. Working with the World Bank, the MMEWR then 'rationalised' the water sector. Since May 2009, users of water have been expected to enter into a water supply agreement with the WUC. To date, 285 villages have been 'taken over' by the WUC for the purposes of potable water service delivery. The WUC takeover of waste-water service delivery will have been completed by 2014.

Concern has been expressed in various quarters about the long-term effect of the revised water service supply on access to water by the poor. Water is a scarce resource and the government's aim is to ensure universal access to safe drinking water. According to the *UN Development Programme Millennium Development Goals Report 2010*, 4% of the population did not have access to safe drinking water in the period reported on. In 1994, this figure was 23%. In 1996, 77% of the population had sustainable access to safe drinking water. In 2000, the figure rose to 97.7%. There have been disparities between urban and rural households: in 2000, nearly all households had running water in their homes or could fetch it from a nearby public standpipe, but only 9.1% of rural households had piped water in their homes. Water is transported in bowsers to settlements in remote areas. Approximately 84.2% had access to public standpipes and about 7% of the rural population did not have access to safe drinking water at all.

A National Water Master Plan was developed in 1991; a set of plans arising from the extensive analysis options for the development and management of water resources of Botswana until 2020. The plan not only outlines basic physical and engineering developments, but also takes into account economic, social, environmental, institutional and legal factors.

Adequate food

Adequate access to nutritious food, as well as water, is essential for the growth, survival and development of any individual. Internationally, the right to food is contained in the UDHR. Article 25 states that 'everyone has the right to a standard of living adequate for the health and well-being of himself and of his family, including food'. Botswana is party to this declaration. The ICESCR recognises 'the right of everyone to an adequate standard of living for himself and his family, including adequate food' (article 11(1)) and 'the fundamental right of everyone to be free from hunger' (article 11(2)). The meaning of these provisions has been clarified by the CESCR in its General Comment No. 12 of 1999. Other General Comments are also relevant to the right to food (e.g. General Comments No. 3 of 1990 and No. 15 of 2000). While not actually binding, general comments constitute the authoritative interpretation of legally binding treaty provisions issued by the UN body responsible for monitoring the application of the treaty. Botswana is not party to this covenant.

The Convention on the Rights of the Child (CRC) recognises 'the right of every child to a standard of living adequate for the child's physical, mental, spiritual, moral and social development' (article 21(1)). The CRC requires States to combat child malnutrition (article 24(2)(c)) and to 'take appropriate measures' to assist parents in fulfilling their primary responsibility to implement children's right to an adequate standard of living, 'particularly with regard to nutrition' (article 27(3)). Botswana is a party to this convention.

The Convention on the Elimination of All Forms of Discrimination Against Women (CEDAW) requires States to ensure that women have 'adequate nutrition during pregnancy and lactation' (article 12(2)) and to 'take all appropriate measures to eliminate discrimination against women in rural areas in order to ensure, on a basis of equality of men and women, that they participate in and benefit from rural development and, in particular ... enjoy adequate living conditions, particularly in relation to housing, sanitation, electricity and water supply, transport and communications' (article 14(2)(h)). Botswana is a party to this convention.

The right to adequate food does not mean that individuals and groups (the 'right holders') have a general entitlement to be provided with food. It is primarily interpreted as the right to feed oneself in dignity, through economic and other activities. In other words, individuals and groups are responsible for undertaking activities that enable them to have access to food. Nonetheless, the State has an important role to play in facilitating these efforts.

Adequate Shelter and Housing

In Botswana, there is no guaranteed right to adequate shelter or housing in urban areas. In rural areas, natural resources for traditional shelter are available, but special licences for harvesting veld products must be obtained in order to access thatching grass for roofing. The high cost of building materials, which are largely imported, makes housing unaffordable to the poor. The market price for purchasing or renting houses is also very high. Particularly in the urban areas, land-use permits have resulted in land scarcity. The Botswana Housing Corporation was set up in 1970 to provide housing and office buildings for the government and local authorities, but the Botswana Housing Corporation Act[8] makes no provision for the right to adequate shelter. The Self-Help Housing Agency (SHHA) scheme provides loans for low-income earners (366 to 3033 Pula per month), but there is no grant for those with no income.

The challenges faced by the poor in accessing adequate shelter and housing are recognised by the president, who has initiated a national housing appeal that draws on financial and in-kind contributions from the private sector and citizens. This scheme had realised the building of 453 houses by November 2011.[9]

ADEQUATE AND UNIMPEDED ACCESS TO LAND

There is no constitutional guarantee of the right to land, but any Motswana can apply for land anywhere in the country, according to the Tribal Land Amendment Act (1993), which provides free access to the services of the land boards and their resources. This framework allows every Motswana to access information about the ownership of specific land. Legislation regarding the administration of land, primarily the State Land Act (1966), the Chieftainship Act (1966), the Customary Law Act (1969) and the Tribal Land Act (1968), also enables all citizens to access land.

The land boards, set up under the Tribal Land Act (1968), play an important role in ensuring adequate and unimpeded access to communal land and, therefore, customary land rights. However, State land and freehold land are administered through the Department of Lands in the Ministry of Lands and Housing. The separation of these two governing bodies regarding the administration of land is useful for the citizens of Botswana, as each body is able to ensure that the correct procedures are followed regarding the administration of specific categories of land.

The government's policies after independence in 1966 were constructed to enable equitable access to land for all. Prior to these policies, chiefs had allocated and administered land, but the introduction of district councils and land boards allowed the distribution of land to be regulated and opened up access for everyone. Land for customary use in Botswana is defined as residential, grazing or arable, all of which require customary land rights certificates. Concerns with the procedure for accessing land through the land boards include administrative delays and possible corruption. There is anecdotal evidence that applications made in 1993 for the use of tribal land for residential purposes in Mogoditshane, a peri-urban area neighbouring Gaborone, are still pending.

To control the use of land in Botswana, limitations were applied by the Tribal Grazing Land Policy of 1975. This policy was introduced to encourage commercialisation of the livestock industry and allowed cattle owners access to leasehold farms on communal lands through a procedure known as dual grazing. However, a problem highlighted through the implementation of this policy appeared to be overgrazing by those with power and, therefore, an imbalance among those using the communal lands. The National Policy on Agricultural Development, formulated in 1991, was also aimed at enabling the agricultural use of land. This policy was designed to enable borehole owners collectively to fence off grazing areas, but became a problem as it infringed the rights of pockets of indigenous peoples living on communal land, who were evicted once the title changed to communal leasehold as they no longer had the right to reside on that land.

Currently, if an individual in Botswana wants access to ploughing land, there are formalities that must be followed, such as the purchase of a tender document costing 500 Pula, a prepared business proposal and a certified financial bank statement. This presents a problem, as it excludes those who cannot afford the initial tender and those who are unable to produce a bank statement. This highlights the divide between those who have access to ploughing land and those who do not, depending on their financial status.

Gender equality in the acquisition of land has become a prominent issue through the Abolition of Marital Power Act (2004), which enabled women to acquire and transfer their own land.

Health Care

85. To what extent is the right to adequate health care protected in all spheres and stages of life? Is treatment available for illnesses such as HIV/Aids? Is access to treatment equitable? (6)

As noted above, the Constitution of Botswana does not guarantee the right to health care. The provision of health care in Botswana is guided by the Public Health Act.[10] The regulation of health care professionals is governed by the Botswana Health Professions Act[11] and the Nurses and Midwives Act.[12]

The government has adhered to standards set by the World Health Organisation with regard to access to clinics in terms of geographic distance in relation to recognised settlements. An estimated 95% of the population has access to a health facility within a radius of 8 km.

Public health care is also accessible in terms of cost, in that citizens can access the highest level of specialist services at minimal cost. The major challenge for public health care, in contrast to private health care – and this is something that calls into question the efficacy of public health care – is the issue of time delays in accessing specialised services. There are also concerns regarding the efficiency of health care service providers, and there have been media reports of cases of incorrect HIV diagnosis and wrong prescriptions being issued.

Botswana is one of the countries hardest hit by the HIV/Aids epidemic. Life expectancy has declined by more than ten years due to the epidemic, with the expectancy in 1970 being 54 years, compared to 43.2 years in 2002 (Aids and Human Rights Research Unit 2007). The general challenges in the public health care system exacerbate the HIV/Aids epidemic in particular. The Botswana Network on Ethics, Law and HIV/Aids (BONELA) litigated on behalf of Kgakamatso Sekgabetlela in a case of wrongful diagnosis against the government of Botswana. This was a case of negligence and the plaintiff sued for 500 000 Pula. The case set a legal precedent, not only in Botswana and regionally, but also internationally.

Judgment was handed down on 29 October 2009 by Justice Key Dingake. The judge stated that the plaintiff had been traumatised by the incorrect HIV-positive test result, to the extent that she was later diagnosed with post-traumatic stress disorder and at one point contemplated suicide due to her inevitable mental anguish.

Table 5.1: Child mortality and maternal health statistics in Botswana					
Goals	Target	Indicator	1990	2003	2007
Reduce child mortality	Reduce by two-thirds between 1990 and 2015 the under five mortality	Under five mortality	57.0		76.0
		Infant mortality rate (per 1 000 births)	48.0		57.0
		Proportion of one-year-old children immunised against measles	45.0		90.0
Improve maternal health	Reduce by three quarters the mater-nal mortality ratio	Proportion of births attended by skilled health personnel	77.0	96.1	94.6
		Maternal mortality rate (100 000)	326		193
Source: ROB & UN 2010:18.					

As Table 5.1 indicates, the government of Botswana has taken steps to reduce infant mortality and maternal morbidity, which are critical targets of the millennium development goals. Initiatives taken to reduce child mortality have not had the effect anticipated, owing to variables such as the HIV/Aids epidemic. In 1990, under-five mortality was 57.0 per 1 000 live births, but in 2007 it increased to 76.0. During the same period, access to and acceptance of immunisation campaigns increased, as is evident from the doubling in the proportion of one-year-old children immunised against measles between 1990 and 2007.

In 2001, Botswana became the first country in Africa to offer its citizens free antiretroviral therapy (ART) in the public health system. This service is still available. There is concern that vulnerable people in Botswana under the jurisdiction of the government, such as prisoners of foreign nationality, are not provided with free ART. The director of BONELA, Mr Uyapo Ndadi, has stated: 'The government of Botswana is subjecting inmates to inhumane and degrading treatment contrary to the Constitution of Botswana.'

The Prisons Act[13] provides in Parts VII and VIII for prisoners to receive prompt and appropriate medical treatment at all times. The Prisons HIV and Aids Policy also states in clause 12.1 that the standard of care for people living with HIV/Aids (PLWHA) in prison will be no less than that provided for PLWHA in the general community. The policy further provides that care and treatment for HIV/Aids is to be dispensed without compromising the rights of infected prisoners to confidentiality and non-discrimination.

The practical implementation of these policy provisions has been questionable. According to BONELA, the following concerns have been reported:

• Infected prisoners are stigmatised by prison officers and other inmates.

• There are various defects in the procedure and practice of HIV/Aids care.

• Care for the infected is not a priority for health officers, and prisoners care for their fellow inmates with no standard protective gear and no medical training.

• Officers delay dispensing medication, with the result that infected prisoners miss their doses. This lapse in the dispensation of medication poses a serious threat to effective treatment.

There are, however, instances in which, even though treatment is available to those infected with HIV, there is wilful refusal to take the medication. The Botswana-Baylor Children's Clinic, a paediatric HIV/Aids care centre, has reported a few such cases of children, especially teenagers, being non-compliant and refusing to take medication. Parents also deny their children's HIV-positive status and do not allow the children to access adequate care, including access to medication.

The government does not provide recognised refugees and asylum seekers with free ART. They are excluded from the programme and, therefore, remain an untreated group in society (Ditshwanelo 2006:16). However, non-governmental organisations give recognised refugees and asylum seekers living at the Dukwi refugee camp free ART.

Without a doubt, the government is making health care available and accessible to its citizens. However, the failure to entrench the right to health care in the Constitution or to express it in any other law means that there is no guarantee or protection of the right to health care and no protection in the case of any derogation.

Education

86. How extensive and inclusive is the right to education and training, including education on the rights and responsibilities of citizenship? (5)

Article 26 of the UDHR states that 'everyone has the right to education'. According to the former UN Special Rapporteur on the Right to Education, Katarina Tomasevki, for education to be a meaningful right, it must be available, accessible, acceptable and adaptable (Tomasevski 2003: Chapter 4).

The Constitution does not provide for the right to education, but the Children's Act (2009) contains such a right for children under the age of 18. However, there is no regulatory framework or specific budgetary allocation to realise this right. Generally, a piecemeal legislative framework regulates education in Botswana: the Education Act[14] governs education in primary and secondary schools, while vocational training operates in terms of the Vocational Training Act[15] and tertiary examinations are held under the Botswana Examinations Council Act.[16] Efforts are being made to review these Acts and to establish a harmonised framework for legislation on education.

Adult literacy and school enrolment ratios have risen hugely since independence. The adult literacy ratio was 81% in 2003, when the last comprehensive National Literacy Survey was carried out (ROB & UN 2010:20).

While education is free at primary and secondary levels in government schools, the Revised National Education Policy of 2003 provided for the introduction of cost recovery measures for primary and secondary learners. Exemptions are possible in the case of indigent children and children of recognised refugees and asylum seekers.

Education is not compulsory in Botswana, and there are two schools of thought on whether it should be. Challenges in the acceptability, relevance and suitability of the present education system are used by detractors of compulsory education to argue for preserving the present system. The *Report on the Education of Children in the Remote Area Dwellers Programme* supports the view that education should not be made compulsory.

The education sector in Botswana accounts for about 25% of public expenditure. In 2008–2009, education was allocated 8.2% of the development budget and 28.5% of the recurrent budget. In 2009–2010, education accounted for 19.6% of the total budget. This trend has been repeated in the 2011–2012 and 2012–2013 budgets, with both cases showing education getting the largest share of the recurrent budget (Ditshwanelo 2012:1). Investment in education has been increasing at an annual rate of 4% over the past decade. This has resulted in good infrastructure, high teacher-pupil ratios, improved qualifications among national teachers, and improved equipment and materials in schools. In 2009, Botswana had 803 schools, of which 742 were public schools (ROB & UN 2010:26).

The sector has faced a number of challenges over the past two years. These include acrimony in the relationship between teachers' representative organisations and officials in the Ministry of Education and Skills Development. Differences of opinions about conditions of service in 2010 led to teachers withdrawing their services for extra-curricular activities, invigilation and marking of examination scripts. This resulted in a delay of more than three months in the release of examination results. Students who had successfully completed Form 3 (the tenth year in Botswana's K–12 education system) were only able to take up their places in Form 4 in April 2011 instead of January, meaning that four months of instruction was lost.

The eight-week public sector strike also negatively affected the education sector in 2011. During the strike (April to June 2011) teachers withdrew their services from schools. At the end of the strike, they refused to cover material which should have been taught during the period they were absent from classes as long as the government upheld the principle of not paying teachers for work they had failed to carry out due to the strike. Negotiations between the teacher organisations and the Ministry of Education and Skills Development resulted in various strategies being put in place to make up for the work not covered.

While the infrastructural framework exists for the general delivery of education, a one-size-fits-all approach is being applied. The education sector has failed to take into account the variables among the various segments of the population, which detracts from the inclusivity of the education provided.

POVERTY

87. Are vulnerable groups such as children, people with disabilities and women adequately protected from poverty? (4)

88. How much impact on political participation does poverty have? How far are poor people able to participate in the wider Botswana society? To what extent are they excluded? (5)

89. To what extent is the State 'progressively realising' these social and economic rights in accordance with its constitutional obligations?　(6)

The Constitution does not provide for the protection of vulnerable groups from poverty. The government has instituted a National Poverty Eradication Programme, which is being co-ordinated by the Office of the President. Prior to this initiative, the 2002 National Strategy for Poverty Reduction coordinated all efforts with regard to poverty in the Ministry of Finance and Development Planning (MFDP). These initiatives include the Remote Area Development Programme, which targets predominantly disadvantaged minorities and indigenous people, the Basarwa/San, living in remote areas. The old age pension also provides income support for those aged above 65. The Destitute Programme provides support to the indigent generally, and the Orphans Programme assists children who have lost one or both parents. The Integrated Support Programme for Arable Agricultural Development provides inputs to farmers, including those who are resource-poor. Schemes such as Destitute Housing, SHHA, Ipelegeng, youth funding programmes, the Citizen Entrepreneurial Development Agency (CEDA) and the Local Enterprise Authority (LEA) help the poor leverage resources to get out of poverty. Unfortunately, many disadvantaged groups, such as people with disabilities, have indicated that the requirements to participate in CEDA and LEA programmes exclude people with disabilities and, in fact, aggravate their economic marginalisation.

The wide-ranging social safety nets outlined above ensure that the food needs of those most vulnerable to hunger and malnutrition are met. The main target groups include destitute persons, orphans, and PLWHA (ROB & UN 2010:20). There are indications that, as a result of these initiatives, the basic needs of the majority of Batswana are met. However, the absence of guarantees in the Constitution means that if these socio-economic provisions cease to be provided, the beneficiaries do not have grounds to litigate. Furthermore, many critics note that the existing social safety nets invariably fail to graduate recipients from poverty.

Within Botswana, formal unemployment was estimated at 26.2% in 2008 as compared to 17.6% in 2005. Unemployment is especially high among the youth, and it is estimated that 19% of the population depends on one type of welfare scheme or another (ROB and UN 2010:20). Causes of vulnerability to poverty have been identified, which include HIV/Aids, adverse climatic conditions and climate change (ROB & UN 2010:20). Geographic factors also play a role: rural areas, south-western Botswana in particular and remote areas in general have a higher incidence of poverty.

As meaningful participation in political activity requires finance and there is no State funding of political parties in Botswana, people with disabilities and the poor are not able to participate fully in political activity. While there are economic factors behind non-participation, there are also issues of self-esteem and gender stereotyping that prevent the meaningful participation of women in political activity. Non-governmental organisations such as Emang Basadi and the Women's Information Centre are working with the Department of Women's Affairs in the Ministry of Labour and Home Affairs to empower women to take action to increase their participation in political leadership.

Jobs and Rights in the Workplace

90. Is there equal opportunity for all, irrespective of ethnicity, in the workplace? (6)

91. How far are workers' rights to fair rates of pay, just and safe working conditions and effective representation guaranteed in law and practice? (4)

92. How far are wage levels and social security or other welfare benefits sufficient for people's needs, without discrimination (equally)? (2)

The main legal framework regulating the workplace in Botswana is the Employment Act.[17] Freedom of association and collective bargaining are supported by the Trade Unions and Employers' Organisations Act[18] and the Trade Disputes Act.[19] In addition, the government has ratified the major International Labour Organisation (ILO) conventions (87, 98, 135, 151 and 154) dealing with freedom of association and the right to collective bargaining.

However, the major trade unions under the Botswana Federation of Public Sector Unions undertook strike action from April to June 2011 after wage increase negotiations with the government had failed. Tensions arose over the right of certain categories of workers to strike. The government amended the law that regulates the sectors classified as essential workers to include more categories of workers. Essential services workers are not allowed to strike, so a number of employees were dismissed as a result of 'illegal strike action' and a number of cases arising are pending before the Industrial Court and the High Court.

There is no data on how ethnicity influences unemployment or employability, except in so far as some groups might not maximise the benefits of free education and might thus, owing to their lack of formal education, be less employable.

Delivery of Social and Economic Rights

93. Are public goods, for example water provision or local services such as waste collection, equally available to citizens and communities at similar levels of efficiency and competence? (4)

94. To what extent has privatisation had an impact on the adequate provision of public goods and services? (3)

95. To what extent do public-private partnerships or does privatisation facilitate or impede access to socio-economic rights, particularly for the poor? (3)

96. To what extent are private companies accountable for the delivery of socio-economic rights as a result of privatisation or public-private partnerships? To what extent is this accountability overseen by citizens or their representatives? (0)

97. To what extent do citizens feel they are receiving equal access to public resources regardless of their social grouping? (8)

In a survey conducted among Batswana in 2008, respondents were asked: 'How well or badly would you say the current government is handling or managing the economy, or haven't you heard enough to say?' More than three quarters (76%) of respondents rated the government as doing fairly well or very well. This was in contrast to 2003, when only 60% gave the government positive marks (Lekorwe 2009).

While sanitation and other public goods are available in Botswana, challenges exist in terms of access and efficiency. The local authorities are responsible for waste collection. While service provision in this regard is fairly reliable in urban areas, in rural areas communities experience challenges in accessing services, resulting in environmentally unsound and unsustainable strategies being employed for the disposal of waste.

Consultations with the government authorities reveal that, although the Public Enterprises Evaluation and Privatisation Agency is in place, public-private partnerships are not widespread or proven to be successful.

The private sector relies on the government for tenders to support government-led service delivery rather than being an engine of economic growth. The Botswana Confederation of Commerce, Industry and Manpower has committed itself to the advancement of citizen-led companies and is involved in the High Level Consultative Council (HLCC), which is chaired by the president. The HLCC meets twice a year and brings together senior representatives of the government, the private sector and additional key stakeholders, including civil society organisations such as the Botswana Council of Non-Governmental Organisations (BOCONGO). The work of the HLCC is supported by economic sub-sector committees in all ministries.

CORPORATE GOVERNANCE

98. How rigorous and transparent are the rules on corporate governance? And how effectively are corporations regulated in the public interest? (3)

99. To what extent are companies duty-bound to play a role in the realisation of socio-economic rights? And to what extent do they prioritise responsible social investment? (3)

100. Is the private sector meeting its new obligations, such as in relation to equity and empowerment responsibilities? (3)

At present, the Companies Act[20] provides the framework for corporate governance. While the Act increases corporate transparency and the accountability of directors, there is an inadequate regulatory framework to monitor compliance. Social investment is dependent on the management of each particular company and is not adequately guided or harnessed to have a sustainable impact on general socio-economic advancement. The corporate sector is involved in charity handouts of blankets and food packages to vulnerable groups such as the elderly, the poor, and orphans and vulnerable children. A few companies, such as Debswana, First National Bank, Barclays Bank and Standard Chartered Bank, provide support to non-governmental organisations to help them meet their developmental targets, but this is not based on a legal or regulatory framework.

CONCLUSION AND RECOMMENDATIONS

In Botswana, services are provided because it is 'the right thing to do', not because they are recognised as rights to be progressively realised. While health and education alone consistently account for over a third of the national budget, the development paradigm has to shift to a 'people-centred' approach to development.

People-centered development is an approach to international development that focuses on improving local communities' self-reliance, social justice, and participatory decision-making. It recognises that economic growth does not inherently contribute to human development and calls for changes in social, political, and environmental values and practices (Korten 1984:341).

The failure to domesticate international and regional human rights commitments into the laws of Botswana, and the absence of a constitutional framework guaranteeing socio-economic rights, detract from the efficacy of the access to services and opportunities that citizens enjoy in Botswana. This will impact on sustainability, as there is general uncertainty as to whether a policy shift that is less favourable to the poor and vulnerable can be prevented by the courts, which are the guardians of human rights and human dignity. This uncertainty goes to the core of the sustainability of Botswana's form of democracy.

Given the circumstances, the government needs to become a State party to the ICESCR. There is also a need to incorporate economic, social and cultural rights into the Constitution, and to develop strategies that empower vulnerable groups in society. These steps would provide a basis for the progressive, sustainable realisation of socio-economic rights in Botswana. They would also allow economic, social and cultural rights to be guaranteed in Botswana.

ENDNOTES

1 A Setswana term referring to the humaneness of a person.

2 http://www.moibrahimfoundation.org/en/media/get/20111003_ENG2011-IIAG-ScoresTable.pdf.

3 *Matsipane Mosetlhanyane, Gakenyatsiwe Matsipane and further applicants v Attorney-General of Botswana,* Court of Appeal Civil Appeal No. CACLB-074-10 – High Court Civil Case No: MAHLB – 00393-09 January 2011.

4 *Matsipane Mosetlhanyane, Gakenyatsiwe Matsipane and further applicants v Attorney-General of Botswana,* Court of Appeal Civil Appeal No. CACLB-074-10 – High Court Civil Case No: MAHLB – 00393-09 January 2011.

5 http://www.un.org/News/Press/docs/2001/sgsm7738.doc.htm.

6 *Matsipane Mosetlhanyane, Gakenyatsiwe Matsipane and further applicants v Attorney-General of Botswana,* Court of Appeal Civil Appeal No. CACLB-074-10 – High Court Civil Case No: MAHLB – 00393-09 January 2011.

7 Laws of Botswana, CAP 74:02.

8 Laws of Botswana, CAP 74:03.

9 *Daily News*, 10 February 2010, No. 027:4.

10 Laws of Botswana, CAP 63:01.

11 Laws of Botswana, CAP 61:02.

12 Laws of Botswana, CAP 61:03.

13 Laws of Botswana, CAP 21:03.

14 Laws of Botswana, CAP 58:01.

15 Laws of Botswana, CAP 47:04.

16 Laws of Botswana, CAP 48:03.

17 Laws of Botswana, CAP 47:01.

18 Laws of Botswana, CAP 48:01.

19 Laws of Botswana, CAP 48:02.

20 Laws of Botswana, CAP 42:01.

BIOGRAPHICAL INFORMATION

Karin Alexander runs Idasa's strategic team on Measuring and Monitoring Democracy and is a member of the Ibrahim Index on African Governance Advisory Council. A Zimbabwean Rhodes Scholar with an MPhil in Development Studies from Oxford University and an undergraduate degree from Harvard University, her areas of specialisation include democratisation, governance and conflict management. Karin co-wrote *Oil and Governance Report: A Case Study of Angola, Chad, Gabon and São Tomé and Principe* and co-edited *Peace in the Balance: The Crisis in Sudan*, published by the Institute for Justice and Reconciliation, and produced 'Peace Beyond Justice', an educational documentary on the Gacaca Courts in Rwanda. Idasa's States in Transition Observatory (under her management) regularly produces publications including *Developing a Transformation Agenda for Zimbabwe* and monthly Election Watch monitoring reports on key SADC states.

Gape Kaboyakgosi holds a doctorate in Public Policy from the Australian National University, Canberra, where he specialised in the field of regulation. He is currently acting head of the Public Sector Reforms Unit at the Botswana Institute for Development Policy Analysis. His research interests include government-business relations, governance, and public policy and administration.

Dr **Emmanuel Botlhale** is a senior lecturer in Public Finance in the Department of Political Science and Administrative Studies at the University of Botswana. His teaching and research interests are: public budgeting, fiscal federalism, financial administration, project management, research methods and governance. He has published in journals including: *Development Southern Africa, Journal of Social Policy and Society, Research in Applied Economics, Perspectives: a public governance journal* and *Journal of Public Administration and Governance.*

Keneilwe P. Marata holds an MPhil in Public Policy and Administration (Democratic Governance) from the University of Cape Town. She obtained her Bachelor of Arts degree from the University of Botswana, majoring in Public Administration and Political Science. She is an associate researcher at the Botswana Institute for Development Policy Analysis. Keneilwe is co-author of 'Beyond Public Administration? HIV/AIDS Policy Networks and the Transformation of Public Administration in Botswana', published in a Public Administration and Development journal in 2008. Her research interests include public sector reforms and public policy analysis, democratic governance and traditional authorities in modern Africa.

Ingrid Melville, a lawyer and international development practitioner, has worked in promoting good governance with organisations such as the UN Development Programme and the UN Volunteers Programme. She participated in service delivery transformation within Southern Africa through the Southern Africa Capacity Initiative. After leading governance and HIV and AIDS interventions with the Parliament of Lesotho, Ingrid helped shape the human rights infrastructure in Botswana when she worked at Ditshwanelo – the Botswana Centre for Human Rights between 1999 and 2012. She holds a post-graduate Legal Education Certificate from the Hugh Wooding Law School, Trinidad.

Segametsi Oreeditse Moatlhaping is country project manager of a European Union and Swedish International Development Agency funded project at the Botswana Association of Local Authorities. She has worked in the Office of the President – Public Service Reforms Unit as principal management analyst. She has provided policy advice on issues related to public administration reforms, governance, sustainability, service improvement, financial management, local economic development and strategy management to Office of the President, government ministries, municipalities, businesses and other stakeholders. She co-facilitated the drafting of Chapter 12 of *National Development Plan 10*, which focuses on key areas of Open and Transparent Governance in Botswana. Segametsi, who holds an MPhil in Sustainable Development, Planning and Management from Stellenbosch University and a Master of Arts in Development Studies from the University of Botswana, has also served as a board member of various local and international institutions.

Alice Mogwe is the director of Ditshwanelo – The Botswana Centre for Human Rights. She studied law at the University of Cape Town and the University of Kent and has worked on human rights issues since 1990. She is a board member of national, regional and internation organisations that focus on poverty eradication, human rights and the creation and strengthening of open, democratic societies.

Gaontebale Mokgosi is the manager of New Hope Youth Trust, which focuses on promoting good practice in youth participation. He is also the coordinator of BOCONGO Youth sector. He holds a diploma in Public Relations from the Institute of Commercial Management in Bournemouth, England, and his areas of specialisation include promoting democratic principles and youth participation, project development and management. Gaontebale has had 13 years of experience in the NGO sector where he has initiated, implemented, monitored and evaluated youth leadership programmes. He was instrumental in the development of the Botswana Youth Charter and the launch of the Botswana Youth Parliament in 2003. Gaontebale is a member of the ABM University Council and the Botswana Examinations Council Research Board.

Ketlhomilwe Moletsane has been the executive secretary of the Botswana Association of Local Authorities since 2008. Among his responsibilities are to ensure that the association has a clear strategic focus on sustainable development and advancing the interests of the poor in Botswana. Before that, he worked for the Botswana Council of Non-Governmental Organisations.

Thapelo Ndlovu is publisher and editor-in-chief of *Sniffdog* news magazine. A media and civil society activist, Thapelo was the national director of the Media Institute of Southern Africa, Botswana chapter, and is currently the chairperson of Botswana Council of Non-Governmental Organisations. He has had analytical articles published on various international websites such as Committee to Protect Journalists, Free African Media and Think Africa Press. He contributed analysis to the Media Institute of Southern Africa's *2011 So This is Democracy* annual publication.

References

ACEMOGLU, D., JOHNSON, S. & ROBINSON, J. 2003. 'An African success story: Botswana' in Rodrik, D. (ed.) *In search of prosperity: Analytic narratives on economic growth*. Princeton, NJ: Princeton University Press, 80–119.

AIDS AND HUMAN RIGHTS RESEARCH UNIT. 2007. *Human rights protected: Nine southern African country reports on HIV, Aids and the law*. Pretoria: Pretoria University Law Press (PULP).

AMBERT, C. 2000. *Participatory processes for municipal planning in post-apartheid South Africa*. Johannesburg: University of the Witwatersrand. Available: http://www.wits.ac.za/urbanfutures/papers/ambert.htm.

ANON. n.d.a 'The presidency of General Ian Khama: Militarisation of the Botswana "Miracle"' [online]. Available: http://bit.ly/H39CDu.

___ n.d.b 'The presidency of General Ian Khama' [online]. Available: http://www.iankhama.com.

___ n.d.c 'Kalafatis killers bail pending appeal fails' in *Weekend Post*. Available: http://bit.ly/H4NVkb.

___ 2009. 'Law Society to petition Khama' in *The Botswana Gazette*, 29 September 2009. Available: http://bit.ly/H39Vy4.

BAAITSE, F. 2010. 'Flogged Mochudi woman loses her baby' in *The Voice*, 15 October 2010.

BALA. 2000. *Botswana: A guide to effective council leadership in the 21st century*. Gaborone: Botswana Association of Local Authorities.

___ 2007. *Mapping local democracy*. Gaborone: Botswana Association of Local Authorities.

___ 2009. *Mapping local democracy*. Gaborone: Botswana Association of Local Authorities.

___ 2010. *Mapping local democracy*. Gaborone: Botswana Association of Local Authorities.

BALISE, J. 2011. 'DCEC pounces on BDC amid alleged corruption reports' in *Sunday Standard*, 3 October 2011: 5.

BALULE, T. & MARIPE, B. 2000. *A guide to laws and practises that inhibit freedom of expression in Botswana*. Gaborone: Media Institute for Southern Africa.

BAPUTAKI, C. 2011. 'Khama rejects meeting with unions over strike'in *Mmegi*, 15 April 2011:1.

BIDPA. 2010. *Presentation of the Open Budget Index Survey*. Gaborone: Botswana Institute for Development Policy Analysis.

BOCONGO, IMPACT ALLIANCE & IDASA. 2008. *Local Governance Barometer Report, February*. Botswana Council of Non-Governmental Organisations, Impact Alliance, Idasa (unpublished).

BONELA & LeGaBiBo. 2008. *The violations of the rights of lesbian, gay, bisexual and transgender persons in Botswana*. Botswana Network on Ethics, Law and HIV/Aids, and Lesbians, Gays and Bisexuals of Botswana.

BOPA NEWS. 2000. 'Globalisation demands sound leadership – Speaker', 26 June 2000. Available: http://bit.ly/GQv7Uf.

BOTLHALE, E.K. 2010a. *Getting into the blackbox: Fiscal decentralisation, popular participation and local government performance in Botswana.* Saarbrücken: VDM.

___ 2010b. 'Democratising the budgetary process in Botswana' in *Journal of Social Policy and Society,* 5(2):85–93.

___ 2011a. 'Freedom of Information Act and transparency' in *The Botswana Gazette,* 4–10 May 2011:25.

___ 2011b. 'A quest to run the government by black ink in Botswana in 2012 and beyond' in *Journal of Public Administration and Governance,* 1(1):24–41.

BOTLHOMILWE, M.Z., SEBUDUBUDU, D. & MARIPE, B. 2011. 'Limited freedom and intolerance in Botswana' in *Journal of Contemporary African Studies,* 29(3):331–348.

BOTSWANA CONGRESS PARTY. n.d. Democracy Alert [online]. Available: http://www.bcp.org.bw.

___ 2011. 'Police refuses to grant opposition permit to hold peaceful march' (press release), 14 May 2011. Available: http://bit.ly/H3awzR.

BUREAU OF DEMOCRACY, HUMAN RIGHTS, AND LABOR. 2010. *2009 Human rights report: Botswana.* Washington, DC: US Department of State. Available: http://1.usa.gov/GNFaZR.

BURGIS, T. 2009. 'Transcript: FT interview with President of Botswana' in *Financial Times,* 9 March 2009. Available: http://on.ft.com/H6OFVj.

CABRI. 2008. *Budget practices and procedures in Africa.* Pretoria: Collaborative Africa Budget Reform Initiative.

CESCR. 2003. *Report on substantive issues arising in the implementation of the International Covenant on Economic, Social and Cultural Rights.*

CHANZA, N. & SYLVESTER, J. 2010. 'Human dignity and democracy' in Misra-Dexter, N. & February, J. (eds) *Idasa's Democracy Index: Testing democracy: Which way is South Africa going?* Cape Town: Idasa.

COOK, A. & SARKIN, J. 2008. 'Is Botswana the miracle of Africa? Democracy, the rule of law, and human rights versus economic development' in *Transnational law & contemporary problems,* 19(3):453. Available: http://bit.ly/GZ8oZN.

CORKERY, J. (ed.) 1999. *Governance: Concepts and applications.* Brussels: International Institute of Administrative Sciences.

DE BEER, F. 2000. *Participatory development management and RDP.* Cape Town: Juta.

DEMOCRACY RESEARCH PROJECT (University of Botswana). 2002. *Voter apathy report.* Gaborone : Independent Electoral Commission.

DITSHWANELO. 2006. *Shadow report to United Nations Committee on the Elimination of Racial Discrimination.* Gaborone: Ditshwanelo–Botswana Centre for Human Rights. Available: http://bit.ly/GRn75I.

___ 2012. *Report on the 2011/2012 and 2012/2013 Botswana budget*. Gaborone: Ditshwanelo–Botswana Centre for Human Rights.

EDGE, W. 1998. 'Botswana: A developmental State?' in Edge, W. & Lekorwe, M. (eds) *Botswana: Politics and society*. Pretoria: JL van Schaik: 333–348.

GABATHUSE, R. 2011. 'Private media comes under attack at congress' in *The Monitor*, 11 July 2011. Available: http://bit.ly/ruFniL.

GABZ FM 96.2. 2011. 'Public officers ordered to boycott MISA Awards', 28 September 2011. Available: http://bit.ly/GQ2t8K.

GABZ FM NEWS. 2011. 'Kgosi denies his spy unit was involved in extra-judicial killings', 30 June 2011. Available: http://bit.ly/GNFsQx.

GALEITSE, T. 2011a. 'Striking essential workers dismissed' in *The Botswana Gazette*, 18 May 2011:1.

___ 2011b. 'BOFEPUSU sets up a trust fund' in *The Botswana Gazette*, 25 May 2011:1.

GOOD, K. 1996. 'Authoritarian liberalism: A defining characteristic of Botswana' in *Journal of Contemporary African Studies*, 14(1).

GOVERNMENT OF BOTSWANA. 2002. *National policy for non-governmental organisations*. Gaborone: Ministry of Labour and Home Affairs.

GRYNBERG, R. & MOTSWAPONG, M. n.d. 'SACU revenue sharing formula: Towards a developmental agreement'. Forthcoming BIDPA working paper.

HERITAGE FOUNDATION. 2009. 'Botswana' in *2009 Index of Economic Freedom*. Available: http://www.heritage.org/index/country/Botswana.

IEC. 2010a. *2009 General elections national stakeholders evaluation workshop report*. Gaborone: Independent Electoral Commission.

___ 2010b. *Performance audit of the Independent Electoral Commission in respect of the Botswana 2009 general elections*. Gaborone: Independent Electoral Commission.

IFEX. 2001. 'High Court declares advertising ban against newspapers unconstitutional', *International Freedom of Expression Exchange*, 28 September 2001. Available: http://bit.ly/GS4aUD.

KABOYAKGOSI, G. 2003. 'Botswana: The hopes and fears of consolidation' in Doxtader, E. & Villa-Vicencio, C. (eds), *Through fire with water: The roots of division and the potential for reconciliation in Africa*. Cape Town: David Philip.

___ 2011. *Enhancing public budget transparency in Botswana: Why and how?* Gaborone: BIDPA Policy Brief No. 10.

KAUL, M. 2000. *An outsider's inside view: Management reforms in government: A review of international practices and strategies*. London: CAPAM & COMSEC.

KAUNDA, J.M. 2008. *The progress of good governance in Botswana 2008 – Final report of the UNECA project measuring and monitoring progress towards good governance in Africa: The*

African Governance Report II (AGR II). Gaborone: Botswana Institute for Development Policy Analysis; Bay Publishing.

KEKIC, L. 2007. *The Economist Intelligence Unit's index of democracy*. Available: http://econ.st/ep2Z1S.

KELEBONYE, G. 2010. 'BDP-De Beers sleaze: Finally a secret told' in *Mmegi*, 25 February 2010:1.

KEORENG, E. 2011. 'Democracy? What democracy?' in *Mmegi Online*, 27 September 2011. Available: http://bit.ly/H4ZMin.

KGALEMANG, T. 2011. 'Court Orders P373,800 for ex-councillor' in *The Monitor*, 28 February 2011. Available: http://bit.ly/GQD4ss.

KHAMA, I. 2008a. Botswana Pres. Khama's inauguration speech & the 4Ds. Diamonds.net by Rapaport. Available: http://bit.ly/HaCpTX.

___ 2008b. '2008 Independence Day message' in *Tautona Times*, No. 30 of 2008, 4 October 2008. Gaborone: Office of the President.

___ 2010. *State of the Nation address to the second session of the tenth parliament: Delivering people-centred development*, 8 November 2010. Gaborone: Government Printer.

___ 2011. *State of the Nation address to the seventh session of the tenth parliament: Botswana first*. 7 November 2011. Gaborone: Government Printer.

KORTEN, D.C. 1984. 'Strategic organisation for people-centered development' in *Public Administration Review*, 44(4):341–352.

LE ROUX, W. 1999. *Torn apart: San children as change agents in a process of acculturation – A report on the educational situation of San children in southern Africa*. Windhoek, Namibia: Capital Press.

LEKORWE, M. 1989. 'The Kgotla and Freedom Square: One-way or two-way communication?' in Holm, J. & Molutsi, P. (eds) *Democracy in Botswana*. Columbus: Ohio University Press: 216–230.

___ 2009. *Perspectives on economic management in Botswana: Jobs and widespread wealth elude even a well-managed economy*. Afrobarometer Briefing Paper No. 62.

LEKORWE, M. & TSHOSA, O. 2005. 'The organisation of elections and institutional reforms' in Maundeni, Z. (ed.) *40 years of democracy in Botswana (1965–2005)*. Gaborone: Mmegi Publishing House.

LEKORWE, M., MOLOMO, M., MOLEFE, W. & MOSEKI, K. 2001. *Public attitudes toward democracy, governance, and economic development in Botswana*. Afrobarometer Working Paper No. 14. Available: http://bit.ly/H4eyCs.

LOANEKA, M. 2003. 'Intergovernmental fiscal relations in Botswana.' Unpublished MA thesis. University of Stellenbosch.

MAGANG, D. 2008. *The magic of perseverance: The autobiography of David Magang*. Gaborone: Centre for Advanced Studies of African Society.

MAIPOSE, G.S. 2008. *Policy and institutional dynamics of sustained development in Botswana*. Washington, DC: International Bank for Reconstruction and Development & World Bank.

MAKGAPHA, S. 2011. 'BCP, BNF condemn Merafhe's "prestigious award"' in *The Botswana Gazette*, 5 October 2011. Available: http://bit.ly/H6KOcW.

MALUMO, R. 2009. *Botswana: Opposition party reports State media to SADC*. Windhoek, Namibia: Media Institute of Southern Africa. Available: http://bit.ly/GOjP3x.

MASIRE, Q.K.J. & LEWIS, S.R., 2006. *Very brave or very foolish? Memoirs of an African democrat*. Gaborone: Macmillan Botswana.

MATAMBO, K. 2011. *2011/12 Budget speech delivered to the National Assembly on 7 February 2011*. Gaborone: Government Printing and Publishing Services.

MAUNDENI, Z. 2008. 'The Executive' in Maundeni, Z. (ed.) *Transparency, accountability and corruption in Botswana*. Cape Town: Made Plain Communication.

MAUNDENI, Z. (ed.) 2005. *40 Years of democracy in Botswana (1965–2005)*. Gaborone: Mmegi Publishing House. Available: http://bit.ly/H5vWb9.

___ 2008. *Transparency, accountability and corruption in Botswana*. Cape Town: Made Plain Communications.

McELHENNY, S. 2004. 'Minimalist conception of democracy: A normative analysis'. Honors Thesis, New York University. Available: http://bit.ly/GQYfws.

MFDP. 2010. *2011/12 Budget strategy paper*. Gaborone: Ministry of Finance and Development Planning.

___ 2011a. *2012/13 Budget strategy paper*. Gaborone: Ministry of Finance and Development Planning.

___ 2011b. *Revenue pitso briefing paper*. Gaborone: Ministry of Finance and Development Planning.

MFUNDISI, A. 1998. 'The formation and structure of central government and its institutional relationship with local government in Botswana' in Edge, W. & Lekorwe, M. (eds) *Botswana: Politics and society*, Pretoria: JL van Schaik: 162–172.

MISA. 2007. *So this is democracy, 2007*. Windhoek: Media Institute of Southern Africa.

___ 2009a. *African Media Barometer: Botswana 2009*. Windhoek, Namibia: Media Institute of Southern Africa, Friedrich-Ebert-Stiftung. Available: http://bit.ly/H3ndL2.

___ 2009b. 'Duma FM dismisses three employees'. Media Institute of Southern Africa. Available: http://bit.ly/GT358k.

___ 2010. *So this is democracy, 2010*. Windhoek: Media Institute of Southern Africa.

MISA/IFEX. 2009. 'Publishers challenge Media Practitioners Act in court'. International Freedom of Expression Exchange, 11 May 2009. Available: http://bit.ly/H6Lzm7.

MLGL, 1979. *Report of the presidential commission on local government structure in Botswana*. Gaborone: Ministry of Local Government and Lands, Government Printer.

___ 2001. *Report of the presidential commission on local government structure in Botswana.* Gaborone: Ministry of Local Government and Lands, Government Printer.

MOABI, D. 2006. 'Whither Botswana: Abolish the House of Chiefs' in *Mmegi*, 8 June 2006. Available: http://bit.ly/H2lrFd.

MOATLHAPING, S.O.S. 2007. *The role of indigenous governance system(s) in sustainable development: Case of Moshupa Village, Botswana.* Cape Town: Sustainability Institute. Available: http://bit.ly/GOYrt4.

MODIKWA, O. 2011. 'Govt sued over flogging death' in *Mmegi Online*, 6 October 2011. Available: http://bit.ly/H5OXyd.

MODISE, O. & MOSIKARE, O. 2009. 'President versus JSC: lawyers debate' in *Mmegi*, 20 March 2009:4.

MOGAPI, R. 2011. *Government secrecy in an information age: Report on the most open and secret government institutions in Botswana.* Windhoek, Namibia: Media Institute of Southern Africa.

MOENG, G. 2011. 'Language policy discriminates – UB academic' in *Mmegi Online*, 23 September 2011. Available: http://bit.ly/pKxbBd.

MOGAE, F. 2006. 'Mogae takes diamonds for development campaign to the US capital' in *Mmegi*, 13 October 2006:1.

MOLOMO, M. 2005. 'Electoral systems and democracy in Botswana' in Maundeni, Z. (ed), *40 years of democracy in Botswana (1965–2005).* Gaborone: Mmegi Publishing House.

___ 2008. 'Political parties' in Maundeni, Z. (ed.) *Transparency, accountability and corruption in Botswana.* Cape Town: Made Plain Communications.

MOLOMO, M. & SEBUDUBUDU, D. 2005. 'Funding of political parties: Levelling the political playing field' in Maundeni, Z. (ed.) *40 years of democracy in Botswana (1965–2005).* Gaborone: Mmegi Publishing House.

MOLOMO, M.G. 1998. 'The political implications of the 4 October 1997 referendum for Botswana' in *Democratisation*, 5(4):151–175.

___ 2000. 'Democracy under siege: The presidency and executive powers in Botswana' in *Pula: Botswana Journal of African Studies*, 14(1):95–108.

MOLUTSI, P. (ed.) 1989. *Democracy in Botswana.* Gaborone: Macmillan.

MOMPATI, T. & PRINSEN, G. 2000. 'Ethnicity and participatory development methods in Botswana: Some participants are to be seen and not heard' in *Development and Practice*, 10(5):62–37.

MOOKETSI, L. 2007. 'BDF, police sex case set for September' in *Mmegi*, 18 July 2007: 1.

MOREWAGAE, I. 2011a. 'Govt pays P10m to stop spy case' in *Mmegi Online*, 11 March 2011. Available: http://bit.ly/GRHKAt.

___ 2011b. 'Kalafatis killers convicted' in *Mmegi*, 10 June 2011:1.

___ 2011c. 'BOFEPUSU starts "essential services" battle' in *Mmegi Online,* 6 October 2011. Available: http://bit.ly/HaXM5M.

_MOSIKARE, O. 2011. 'Khama, Kgosi "refused" to meet CSIS researcher' in *The Botswana Gazette,* 17 August 2011. Available: http://bit.ly/GRHUYx.

MOTSETA, S. 2011. 'Freedom of Information Act consultations begin' in *The Botswana Gazette,* 19–25 April 2011:1–2.

MOUMAKWA, P.C. 2011. 'The Botswana *kgotla* system: A mechanism for traditional conflict resolution in modern Botswana. Case study of the Kanye Kgotla. Master's thesis, University of Tromsø.

MWAKIKAGILE, G. 2009. *Botswana since independence.* Pretoria: New Africa Press.

NKALA, G. 2008. 'BDP recalls Moatlhodi' in *Mmegi,* 13 November 2008:2.

NOPPEN, D. 1982. *Consultation and non-commitment: Planning with the people in Botswana.* Leiden: African Studies Centre.

NTSABANE, T. 2005. 'Youth and electoral participation in Botswana' in Maundeni, Z. (ed.), *40 years of democracy in Botswana (1965–2005).* Gaborone: Mmegi Publishing House.

NTSABANE, T. & NTAU, C. 2000. 'Youth and electoral participation in Botswana' in *Pula: Botswana Journal of African Studies,* 14(1). Gaborone: Pula Press.

NTSEANE, D. & SENTSHO, J. 2005. 'Women's representation in parliament and council: A comparative analysis' in Maundeni, Z. (ed.), *40 years of democracy in Botswana (1965–2005).* Gaborone: Mmegi Publishing House.

OECD. 2010. *Botswana.* Country Report. Organisation of Economic Cooperation and Development. Available: http://bit.ly/H1BNza.

OMBUDSMAN. 2004. *Report.* Gaborone: Government Printer.

___ 2008. *Annual Report 2008.* Gaborone: Government Printer.

ONTEBETSE, K. n.d. 'Masisi clashes with BONELA over HIV campaign' in *Weekend Post,* 11 December. Available: *http://bit.ly/GQEp6F.*

PHIRINYANE, M. 2005. 'Botswana'in Claassens, M. & Van Zyl, A. (eds) *Budget transparency and participation 2: Nine African case studies.* Johannesburg: Idasa.

PHIRINYANE, M., KAUNDA, J.M., SALKIN, J., KABOYAKGOSI, G., THUPENG, W. & BATSETSWE, L. 2004. *The state of governance in Botswana.* Gaborone: Botswana Institute for Development Policy Analysis.

PHIRINYANE, M., KAUNDA, J.M., SALKIN, J., KABAYAKGOSI, G., THUPENG, W. & KAUNDA, L.B. 2006. *The state of governance in Botswana 2004.* Gaborone: Botswana Institute for Development Policy Analysis.

PICARD, L.A. 1979. 'District councils in Botswana: A remnant of local autonomy' in *Journal of Modern African Studies,* 17(2):285–308.

PIET, B. 2011a. 'be MOBILE implicated in Mokgware case' in *Mmegi Online,* 21 April 2011. Available: http://bit.ly/GQEtzn.

PIET, B. 2011b. 'Democracy loses in front of masses' in *Mmegi*, 17 August 2011:1.

PREECE, J. & MOSWEUNYANE, D. 2003. *Perceptions of citizenship responsibility amongst Botswana youth*. Gaborone: Light Books.

PRESIDENTIAL TASK GROUP. 1997. *Vision 2016: A long-term vision for Botswana: Towards prosperity for all*. Gaborone: Botswana Institute for Development Policy Analysis.

RANTAO, P. 2009. *Why?* Gaborone.

RETENG. 2007. *Alternative report submitted to the Human Rights Committee on the International Covenant on Civil and Political Rights (ICCPR)*. Gaborone: RETENG: The Multicultural Coalition of Botswana.

ROB. 1964. *Botswana Penal Code*. Gaborone: Government Printer.

___ 1968. *Electoral Act*. Gaborone: Government Printer.

___ 1997. *Constitution of Botswana*. Gaborone: Government Printer.

___ 2003. *Finance and Audit Act*. Gaborone: Government Printer.

___ 2004. *Trade Disputes Act, Act No. 15 of 2004*. Gaborone: Government Printer.

___ 2006. *Poverty and Food Security Monitoring Bulletin 1*. Gaborone: Rural Development Coordination Division, Poverty Strategy Unit, Ministry of Finance and Development Planning, Botswana.

___ 2007a. *Constitution of Botswana*. Gaborone, Government Printers.

___ 2007b. *Poverty and Food Security Monitoring Bulletin 2*. Gaborone: Rural Development Coordination Division, Poverty Strategy Unit, Ministry of Finance and Development Planning.

___ 2008a. *Annual Poverty Report 2007/08*. Gaborone: Food and Poverty Policy Coordination Section, Socio-Economic Policy Sub-Division, Secretariat to the Multi-Sectoral Committee on Poverty Reduction, Ministry of Finance and Development Planning.

___ 2008b. *Public Service Act*. Gaborone: Government Printer.

___ 2009. *Children's Act*. Gaborone: Government Printer.

___ 2010. *National Development Plan 10*. Gaborone: Government Printer.

___ 2011. *Freedom of Information Bill* (No. 23 of 2011). Gaborone: Government Printer.

ROB & UN. 2010. *Botswana: Millennium development goals status report*. Gaborone: Republic of Botswana, United Nations in Botswana.

SCHAPERA, I. 1970. *A handbook of Tswana law and custom*. London: Frank Cass.

SEBUDUBUDU, D. 2008. 'Independent Electoral Commission' in Maundeni, Z. (ed.) *Transparency, accountability and corruption in Botswana*. Cape Town: Made Plain Communication.

SELEKA, T., SIPHAMBE, H., NTSEANE, D., MBERE, N., KERAPELETSWE, C. & SHARP, C. 2007. *Social safety nets in Botswana: Administration, targeting and sustainability*. Gaborone: Botswana Institute for Development Policy Analysis, Lentswe La Lesedi.

SOMOLEKAE, G. 1998. *Democracy, civil society and governance in Africa: The case of Botswana* [online]. Available: http://bit.ly/H6nbRe.

SURVIVAL INTERNATIONAL. n.d. 'Jailed for saying Botswana president "looks like a Bushman"' [online]. Available: http://bit.ly/2TvEd4.

TESHOME B., W. 2009. 'Media and multi-party elections in Africa: The case of Ethiopia' in *International Journal of Human Sciences*, 6(1). Available: http://bit.ly/H8JZvv.

TIBONE, C. 2010. *Closing remarks at the 2011/12 Budget pitso*, 28 October 2010. Gaborone: Ministry of Finance and Development Planning. Available: http://bit.ly/GPrB9P.

TOMASEVSKI, K. 2003. *Education denied: Costs and remedies*. London and New York: Zed Books.

TSIE, B. 1998. 'The State and development policy in Botswana' in Hope, R.K. & Somolekae, G. (eds) *Public administration and policy in Botswana*. Cape Town: Juta & Co: 1–20.

UN. 2007. *Second common country assessment for Botswana: Final report*, 12 December. United Nations System in Botswana. Available: http://bit.ly/GQEVgU.

UNDP. 2010. *Human development report 2010. The real wealth of nations: Pathways to human development*. New York: United Nations Development Programme, Palgrave Macmillan.

UNESCAP. 2010. *What is good governance?* United Nations Economic and Social Commission for Asia and the Pacific. Available: http://bit.ly/agVRH.

UNIVERSITY OF BOTSWANA FACULTY. 2008. *2008 Round 4 Afrobarometer survey in Botswana: Summary of results*. Cape Town: Idasa; Legon-Accra: CDD-Ghana; East Lansing, MI: MSU Department of Political Science. Available: http://bit.ly/H52Rio.

US EMBASSY GABORONE. 2005. 'Constitutional amendment falls short of tribal equality' [online]. Available: http://bit.ly/H4ERro.

UWADIBIE, N.O. 1999. *Decentralisation and economic development in Nigeria: Agricultural policies and implementation*. Lanham, MD: University Press of America.

VAUGHN, O. 2003. *Chiefs, power and social change: Chiefship in modern politics in Botswana, 1880s–1990s*. Asmara, Eritrea: Africa World Press.

VISION COUNCIL. 2009. *Vision 2016 Botswana performance report*. Gaborone: Lentswe La Lesedi.

___ 2010a. *National Vision 2016 Citzen household opinion survey*. Gaborone: National Vision Council.

___ 2010b. *Vision 2016 Botswana performance report*. Gaborone: Lentswe La Lesedi.

WORLD BANK INSTITUTE. 2003–2008. Botswana governance report. Available: http://bit.ly/cbl2o.

WORLD BANK. 2011. *World development report 2011: Conflict, security and development*. Washington, DC: World Bank Publications.